Praise for Upon My Soul

Soul is a term rarely used with precise definition in philosophy, religion, or common life. It is generally regarded as descriptive of an entity related to but distinguishable from the body--the spiritual part of human beings that animates their physical existence and survives death.

Charles W. Ranson Web site BELIEVE Religious Information Source

John Stewart's book inspires us to communicate freely at many levels in order to explore and deepen our relationship. Understanding and nurturing the soul of our relationship and the way it joins our two souls together helps us forge strong healthy connections between the earthy and the transcendent. In so doing we become more alive individually, as a couple and in closer contact with the Soul of the Universe.

Sheena King, B.Sc. PT & Yggy King, M.Sc., soul mates

In his long and creative life, John Stewart has had many successful careers. During a friendship of more than thirty years, we have shared common concerns in the building of community, in theological and psychological concepts of the connectedness of the soul with oneself, with others, with nature, and with God. As John reflects back on his life and the role his soul plays in that journey, he invites each of us to ponder our own sense of connectedness. This book is a fascinating read from an extraordinary man.

Dr. D.J. Macdonald M.D., C.R.C.P., F.R.C.P.(C) Community Psychiatrist, Hanover, Ontario

This is a heartfelt work. An honest accounting and coming to terms with a life lived well and with great devotion to the nature of goodness/wholeness. It is the story of, as might be said in Scotland, a lad o'pairts. John Stewart's enquiry into the idea of soul, from ruminations on his life's journey, reflects the wisdom embodied in many traditions of mythology and arrives at an expression of that wisdom similar to ancient Shambhala/Buddhist Philosophy from Tibet, which holds that if you join heaven, earth and man at a profound level the world becomes a magical place. The narrative portrays the intimacy and richness of a life lived close to the land and the heart. It is a genuinely religious and absorbing set of essays.

Cicely Berglund PhD. Molecular Biologist and Buddhist Practitioner

This is an inspirational text. Inspirational in the sense of challenging the reader to access their own life arch and the places where the numinous divine has touched that life, challenged it and prodded it to its own unique greatness and gift. This soulful little volume invites you to take it to bed and it will be waiting for your eager return when you wake up. John paints his own unique story-skin as a vibrant memoir legacy of his highly unique and Personalist life journey. And, maybe best of all, this book likes to pun, make jokes, and poke fun at itself.

Terrill L. Gibson, Ph.D. Jungian Analyst and Pastoral Psychotherapist. Tacoma Washington

Also by John Stewart

Emotional First Aid Manual

UPON MY SOUL

Understanding Soul
Through One Man's Life Stories

John Thomas Stewart

John T. Stewart

Published by
Para-Professional Associates

Library and Archives Canada Cataloguing in Publication

Stewart, John Thomas, 1922-

Upon my soul : understanding soul through one man's life stories / John Stewart.

Includes bibliographical references.

Issued also in electronic format.

ISBN 978-0-9693091-6-1

1. Stewart, John Thomas, 1922-. 2. United Church of Canada--Clergy--Biography. 3. Soul. I. Title.

BX9883.S74A3 2012   287.9'2092   C2012-902982-3

Contents

PART III

SOUL MONITORS LEARNING

PART IV

SHOW AND TELL THE INTIMATE SOUL

Appendices

Acknowledgements

I am grateful to Amanda Peters of North Vancouver, British Columbia for her professional work as my initial copy editor. Judith King of Baddeck, Nova Scotia did the final check, her keen eye finding those errors that the rest of us missed. Her suggestions improved the clarity of some paragraphs whose meaning was unclear due to the spiral, non-linear nature of reflections. Her son Yossarian King came to the rescue when I was bogged down in document formatting. I am grateful to him for giving the book a professional look, and for his work on the cover design. I owe thanks to June Sutherland for introducing me to John O'Donohue's idea of soul friends. It was her gift that led me to reflect on my journey from a soul perspective. Peers and friends who have encouraged me along my journey of reflecting and producing these essays encouraged me to stay with my vision. There have been members of my own family who provided support. Significantly, there have been the rich times with my wife Lillian as we shared memories that arose from my reflections. The written comments on the back cover by those professionals who have read Upon My Soul prior to publication have affirmed that I was on the right track by defining soul from my life stories. Terry Gibson's foreword is worth reading again and again in reminding us that we are part of a much larger scheme of things than our daily routine.

Thank you everyone.

Foreword

by Terry Gibson

A thing is right when it tends to preserve the integrity, stability, and beauty of the living community.
> *Aldo Leopold*

Memoirs are bridges to the ancestors. They bridge a grounded past to a vital future. They remember dreams of the forebears that seed the gardens of their descendants. And always the medium of this narrative, the vessel of its living sinew is the earth. John's text vibrates with this living ancestral earth in every sentence and inscribed image.

The writing of spiritual memoir is an ancient and almost lost art. The surviving stone fragments of Parmenides, the *Dialogues* of Plato, the *Confessions* of Augustine, Hildegard of Bingen's *Illuminations*, Dame Julian of Norwich's *Revelations*, Carl Jung's *Red Book*, Thomas Merton's *Seven Story Mountain*—a distinguished and ancient lineage. And now this humble, soulful little volume adds its gentle accent to the memoir winds of human spirit blowing through the chambers of our species time and space.

This memoir narrates two lives—the individual's and the Soul's. John believes in the primacy of individual soul—that it survives death. But he also wonders throughout this journey, what is family soul, community soul, earth soul, and he seems to imply that all these versions and visions of soul survive

ii

their deaths and join in to the Great Soul, the Atman, White Buffalo Woman or whatever one calls it. I call it, out of the great mystical traditions of the West, the *Anima Mundi*, the spirit of the world.

This *Anima Mundi* is a shy creature. She lives at the crossroads of life—the moments where we are touched by failure, death, despair, unexpected good fortune, and synchronistic meetings. She touches our lives in that instant just before and after midnight, or at dawn, or at dusk. She is especially fond of pilgrims and nomads, the dispossessed seeking shelter, the refugee, and the exile. She broods over the grieving. She is the compassion-bearing *Anima Mundi* and John's book makes her moments of contact with his life an accessible and moving guide and goad for us to be similarly curious about her comings and goings across our life arch. That is what good memoir accomplishes.

And John finds her taking family road trips, arriving at new camp jobs, entering new doctoral programs, leading new congregations, raising Christmas trees, stoking a pot-bellied stove in a one-room schoolhouse, designing creative family reunions, even making innovative stock market investments.

> *All life is bound to carriers who realize it, and it is simply inconceivable without them. But every carrier is charged with an individual destiny and destination, and the realization of these alone makes sense of life.*
>
> C. G. *Jung*

iii

This is an inspirational text. Not inspirational in the maudlin, grocery-store-line tabloid sense. But inspirational in the sense of challenging the reader to access their own life arch and the places where the numinous divine has touched that life, challenged it, prodded it to its own unique greatness and gift. It is about conscious deepening into the arms of one's authentic destiny, what one calls the soul and its guidance and the increasingly conscious denial of what John calls the tempting demands of "murky soul."

Our culture insists on linear narratives. We like such linearity because it is ordered, our order. It doesn't jump out of its prescribed ruts and catch us off guard, surprise us, shock us, scare us, shake us. The soul, what Jungians call Psyche, reserves her deepest affections for spiral narrative, narratives that go round and round, deeper and deeper. This is a spiral text. It does not move in a straight line. Sometimes, even within a sentence, it circles back upon itself and we have to imagine the connections — an imaging that is always worthwhile. It does not forget itself; it simply associates much wider than the printed word. It goes beyond that word to the world, the true world of soul. That is what inspirational writing does best; when it preaches it becomes a genuine homiletics of the soul. Spiral texting is dream texting. It moves through association, mood, ambiance, insinuation. It especially loves such equally spiral things as earth, beauty, and dream. These are things that John relishes most deeply, so it is not surprising that his text reads best when it spirals most widely.

John talks about his years as a doctoral student in the venerable pastoral psychology program at Boston University. I matriculated in the same program a decade after John and so know that the central guiding curricular vision there was Boston Personalism. A philosophical school with roots all the way back to the world-soul thoughts of Plato (the *Anima Mundi* again), a simple description of this Personalist mode of reflecting on the central mysteries of life is its core affirmation of the unique presence and soul of each human being and the unique connection of that being to the animal and natural world around it. No accident here that a farm boy full of earth-soul love would find his way to Boston's Personalist soul. And Personalism posits that the ultimately inexplicable mystery of the divine is stamped into the irreproducible mystery of each of Her creations. When you read John's memoir you experience the irreproducible mystery of his life cast against the tapestry of human drama, anguish, and joy that is the common background of the Being before whom we all dance our distinct personal choreography. Just as Plains Amerindians used pictoglyphic story-skins to describe their ancestral history, John paints his own unique story-skin as a vibrant memoir legacy of his highly unique and Personalist life journey.

And, maybe best of all, this book likes to pun, make jokes, and poke fun at itself. I once travelled

with John to a therapy biz conference. He and I
shared a room. The television set audio did not work
well, so we decided to turn off the sound entirely to
make up dialogue for the film we were watching. We
were like piece-work-actors in a movie studio
dubbing booth—only our dubbing got more
outrageous and insane with each exchange. The
resulting dubbed film was much improved from the
pedestrian rough cut—x rated but much improved.
We laughed ourselves silly into an exhausted, deep
slumber. John loves humour indeed.

    This soulful little volume invites you to take it to
bed and it will be waiting for your eager return when
you wake up.

> *To be religious is to have a life that flows with the
> presence of the extraordinary.*
>   *Ann Belford Ulanov*

Terry L. Gibson Ph.D.
Jungian Analyst
Pastoral Therapy Associates
Tacoma, WA

Introduction

These essays are intended to provide you with a sequence of images that will portray how one (John Thomas Stewart) attempted to maintain an adequate balance between the spiritual life and the natural life. Faced with the impact on his journey, by the rapid changes in our modern world, he decided to reflect on his life from a soul perspective. These essays provide a portrait of his journey. A significant outcome of the exercise has been an understanding of the meaning of Soul. That outcome is set forth in the third essay. He discovered that his soul played an important role in shaping the journey he travelled. The stories in these essays provide a format intended to encourage you to reflect on and share the stories of your own journey. He writes in the following paragraphs an overview of his experience of reflecting.

The experience of reflecting and writing has been my satisfaction and reward. It is my hope that you will be inspired to set this book aside, and reflect on those images that emerge from the recesses of your mind as you pause to enrich your own journey.

Because of cultural, geographic and social differences, your reflected images may well be quite different than mine. It is my hope that there are sufficient similarities between your reflected images and mine to provide you with meaningful experiences as intense as those recorded here. If such moments happen then soul friends "author and reader" have found each other. The judgment of readers is not being sought either as reward or criticism.

These essays are written against the background of a persistent and sometimes unexpected movement from then to now. My soul was the one stabilizing influence that seemed to be able to discern where my journey would take me into the future. At times neither my heart, mind nor any of the five senses could know what was ahead. My soul has blended the abilities of my mind and senses into one operating unit. My soul has understood and managed the influence of change throughout my journey. There have been occasions when I felt that I had entered a strange place. The change was so sudden that for a few moments I was in a state of confusion.

Working alone for hours, days and even months with my Christmas trees over the past eighteen years has provided time to reflect. The reflections are humbling and bring me down to earth. I remember the support and encouragement I received from fellow workers, professional peers and many volunteers from the several communities where I worked. Several of those volunteers hosted a luncheon at which they paid tribute to my work in the community. In response to their gift all I could say was "It was a two way street." The same sentiment expressed by one volunteer when I thanked him for his support. Don McLean was one of my major supports twenty five years earlier.

Reflecting on those years immediately following my schooling in the little one room Greenwood School I am amazed at the distance between then and now. I could not have imagined, even in my wildest dreams, that my life's journey would lead me to become the person I am today. I never thought that I had the ability to succeed in University or to move on into graduate work at three post graduate institutions, receiving degrees at each one of them.

On those days in the here and now, when I have to struggle to find a once familiar word, I reflect in disbelief. I find it difficult to believe that I stood there before an audience to receive my first degree. How could I know that I would be a leader in establishing new projects: a new Pastoral Charge in the Fredericton Presbytery of the United Church of Canada? To find a property, and establish a Lay Training Centre that would serve the Atlantic Provinces and Bermuda. To eventually move our family across the continent and start up a new project for the United Church of Canada, a Pastoral Counselling Centre. Somewhere in the midst of the West Vancouver Centre project, I was to start the one and only Divorce Lifeline program in Canada, modelled on a Seattle project.

I reflect back over time to those post high school days, before I began university. I stand baffled, thinking that I could not manage such a journey. To take the risks, to believe sufficiently in myself to make the next step, was beyond any appreciation of my ability, either as a scholar, or as a leader to establish new ventures.

The hundreds (literal computation and I stopped the exercise at one hundred) of people who have encouraged, supported and assisted me along the journey stand out in my memories. There is a simple rule of mathematics used in investing that applies here. Invest a sum of money at ten percent, let it grow and it will double in seven years. (The same mathematical principle applies to the negative use of a non renewable resource. If we use up ten per cent of a resource at the same rate it is gone before we know it).

An overview of the journey of my soul provides a story of a progressive build up of support, encouragement, help and love. It is easy for me to remember these people as individuals, and to recall with ease the special gifts they heaped on my soul. My soul has grown because of their support. It seems that my best skill was to utilize all of those gifts, and not let them go to waste. Was this particular skill given to me by the Soul of the Universe? I'm certain that a number of those generous individuals exemplified that particular skill, and I was ready to learn from them. To name just four: Don McLean, my friend and volunteer co-worker. J. J. Creighton, my guide and friend during the ten years at Tatamagouche, a man with a beautiful soul. June Sutherland my student, co worker and friend, who when she was barely eighteen caught me alone in a classroom crying. June approached me saying "It takes a big man to cry". Carolyn Gaily was our office manager and friend whose commitment and fabulous memory helped to build a community service. Each of these persons became soul friends. Two of the four have remained soul friends to this day. I have a keen sense that Don and J. J. are my eternal soul mates, reaching across from another dimension. My last telephone conversation with Don was a twenty minute good bye after his life supports had been removed, just before his soul left his body. I could fill pages with specific information about more than a hundred other individuals and their gifts for my journey.

In the soft light of all the support for and shared joy of my accomplishments there have been very few dark rays of negative light. I have to struggle to recall three instances that linger in my memory.

The input from certain persons indicated deep jealousy buried in somewhat murky souls. One of these jealous souls belonged to a minister who graduated from Pine Hill Divinity Hall a year ahead of me. Another jealous soul belongs to a minister who has difficulty with any competition. She has spoken with a forked tongue about all the degrees I have. One relative has made efforts to probe my more immediate family members regarding my degrees. "John's doctorate isn't really a doctorate, is it?" I have observed personally the depth of her soul's jealousy. My farmer brother Seymour easily slides into competition with me in a number of areas. My sister in law Fern says its jealousy. I see it more as sibling competition. I have no negative feelings in response to his efforts to tease competitive dialogue out of me. I refuse to bite. Sometimes my instinct is otherwise, but to fight would be a blemish on my soul.

In this overview I realize that I've always done more than I ever thought I would. Some days I work around my Christmas trees in disbelief as I think about my journey. With a backpack loaded with fertilizer I stumble over a root. I come crashing down to earth. I get up, recover my balance and return to my thoughts. My sudden connection with the earth brings me to another reality about my journey. Those other souls have been the dominant energy fueling my ambitions, success and satisfaction.

For a time period during the fifth decade of my journey the same themes reasserted themselves in my dreams. These themes provide the threads which weave through the fabric of my soul. One of the recurring dreams reflects the nature of the person whose story is told in these essays.

I'm walking on a steep trail that is on the side of a mountain. The terrain is a mix of trees, ponds and pastures. The surroundings are pleasant throughout the dream. In one meadow-like opening there is a pond that invited me to a skinny dip and a swim. I am naked throughout the remainder of the dream.

After a swim I find myself back on the trail. All of a sudden there is a multi-coloured donkey rushing down the trail toward me. I find myself fascinated by the donkey. It does not avoid me by passing to the side. I experience a childlike delight as the donkey flies up and over me on its downward gallop.

For a short time I seem to be in a deep sleep, yet in the same setting. Suddenly I find myself entering a farm-like house and being greeted by three or more people who are in the kitchen. The individuals are not identifiable. Neither they nor I are embarrassed by my nakedness. One of them leads me into a room where the matriarch of the family lies on a bed, terminally ill. A new theme emerges in my dream. Through shared conversation, I find myself ministering to this woman, listening to her concerns about leaving her family, and being empathic to her pain.

There is a break and a bit more deep sleep. I'm still on the same mountain-like trail moving on to a new location, and a new theme. I find myself lying naked on my back on the lower level of a two level bridge that crosses a bubbling stream. There is a woman lying on the upper level of the bridge. Was she one of the individuals in the kitchen? Her face and bare shoulders seem close to me and her hair hangs down touching my face. We share conversation as if we were old friends. The dream always ends at that point. Could it be that it is not politically correct to record in this essay what would happen next between us? My reflection is that the dream always ended there. The politically correct movement had interfered with my soul's involvement in dream work.

In this dream, my soul is providing a summary covering decades of one person's journey. The themes of my dream will keep reappearing in these essays. My nakedness throughout the dream indicates that my true nature is to be open in sharing the story of my soul, and not influenced by any fear of criticism by those whose cultural mores differ from mine. The dream made it easy to be transparent in writing about the pleasure that has been mine through the earthy and sexual aspect of the journey of my soul.

The mountain-like setting for the dream with the trees, a pond and a trail indicate my soul's bonding with nature. The incident of the multi coloured donkey reflects a childlike delight that has remained with me over eight decades.

The dream reflects the major focus of my career: a ministry of caring for and about people. It was one of listening to their pain, concerns and ambitions, sometimes in new and unexpected circumstances. As I entered the threshold of people's lives I was accepted and welcomed as soul meeting soul.

PART I

SOUL UNDERSTOOD
BY REFLECTING ON A JOURNEY

Essay 1

Surprises When Reflecting

"That above all – to thine own self be true; And it must follow as the night the day."
            Polonius' advice to his son in Hamlet

The personal experience which I have had when reflecting on my life journey can be pictured as movement both emotionally and through time. Both my emotions and my thoughts fluctuate between now and then. At times the emotions have been surprising and powerful. Occasionally the recall back to an earlier time in my life has been sudden. At other times the connection between now and then has been more deliberate and thoughtful. The overall process can best be illustrated in the following experiences that I had on a month long walking and climbing tour.

It was March 2004 while I was with a Ramblers walking group in New Zealand. Early one morning we had climbed a local mountain on a low level walk. At the peak we looked down on a lush valley at the edge of which was a small mining town, long since transformed into a tourist attraction. On the descent I stopped to soak up the essence of a real rainbow which, on reflection, appeared to be an omen for an experience about to happen in the local museum. At the end of the rainbow was the old mining town. I went directly to the museum following my descent from the peak. Moving from the kitchen on through

the bedroom and into the workshop of the museum I
was a young teenager back in Musquodoboit,
Canada. The days of old had suddenly become real in
the here and now. Incidentally a few of the relics were
from Canada.

I roamed through the various sections of the
museum in that old mining town in New Zealand. It
was like being in a time machine that took me back
seven decades. It felt like travelling over a rainbow
from New Zealand to Canada, back into time. In the
here and now I was looking at an old fashioned butter
churn. Over the rainbow to Canada I was watching
my mother pushing the-broom like handle of the
churn up and down making butter for our table. At
another time I was a nine year old boy turning the
handle of the cream separator in our barn on the
farm. The images in the here and now served to
stimulate intense reflected memories.

A few days later we visited a small community
Church. The founders of the Church chose a site at
the edge of a lake. I stood in the chancel looking out
of a large window. I was not prepared for the soul
experience that unfolded. The day was clear
providing a good view of Mount Cook. I was miles
distant from that magnificent mountain. Initially I
was recalling the experience I had the previous day.
Twenty four hours earlier I had been walking into the
base of the mountain buffeted by strong winds and
heavy rain.

As I stood looking out of the window of the
Church, suddenly an old spiritual experience

returned to fill me with pleasant emotions.
Thousands of miles away I was seated in a little
United Church in Pemberton, British Columbia,
Canada. The builders of that Church placed its
foundations so that the congregation could see the
snow covered Mount Currie, miles beyond the
chancel windows. Even more impressive than the
snow covered mountain was the silhouette of the
elderly minister who was leading the service. He was
reading the scripture of the day from the Bible, yet he
had been totally blind for years. His blindness was
the result of exposure to the snow and sun while on
one of those mountains. He was reading from
memory one of the ancient stories of the Bible.

In the here and now of a New Zealand Church I
was receiving a special gift. I was reflecting on
experiences of real significance in my spiritual
journey. Two separate events of spiritual awareness
came together.

Were the soul of nature and my soul working
together as these experiences contributed to my
spiritual growth? In the first image my soul was aided
by the beauty of a rainbow over a lush valley. In the
second the beauty of the snow crested Mount Currie
seen from a Holy place provided a setting for the
meeting of spirit and nature. In each reflected
moment it would seem that my soul was sufficiently
mature to create a blending of past and present.

One other lasting memory of my time in New
Zealand illustrates the intense quality of some
reflections. It is imprinted on the soft disc of my

mind. The picture with all its emotional overtones
was captured during a time frame of three or four
minutes. In the spiritual time of the soul the
experience continues onward to this day. We were
travelling by coach to a place where we would begin
our high level walk for the day. It happened as we
were driving along a narrow gravel road about three
hundred feet up on a cliff that nudged its way out
into a small lake which was about one hundred
hectares in size. I was sitting next to a window on the
lake side of the coach. The surface of the water would
have been in perfect calm. The lake served as a
mirror, capturing the scenery surrounding it. The
reflection on the lake zoomed inward on all the
beauty of the sky, trees, a field dotted with sheep,
colorful rock and majestic hills, all in one perfect
reflection. It seemed that nature was providing an
optical illusion, once again done perfectly. Even Van
Gogh or Rembrandt could not attain this level of
beauty or perfection.

My life story written from a soul perspective is
somewhat like that particular experience. It is a
collection of reflections on various aspects of my soul.
Many of the pictures which emerge tend to be like
that reflection on the water. Even more beautiful than
the actual landscape it reflected. Is this tendency
toward perfection the work of the soul?

Reflection is a work of art. The outcome is not
intended to be accurate, as are the results of scientific
research. The truth of the images and events
remembered is in the everyday wisdom embedded in

the stories. Some of the stories come from experiences that were reported to the author. For the most part they come from the reflected experiences of the author. Other stories in the essays are similar to those portions of family history that have been passed on by word of mouth. They are true, but there is no intent that they will be used as sources for establishing an accurate record of events. They are not court documents intended to preserve the date of a birth, marriage or death.

Very few reflections from the now to the then of my life bring up dark nights of the soul. At eighty eight, comparing my life's journey to the journeys of individuals whom I have counseled, I am more than grateful. Either the dark nights of my soul have been few and far between, or else I have developed a way of denying my dark nights, so that they do not arise in reflection.

The story of my soul demonstrates a balance between the three dimensions of a mentally healthy individual. On the one part is my relationship with people. Another part involves my work, productivity and commitment. The third portion of the balanced journey is the pleasure enjoyed and monitored by my soul. There's more later about my soul and pleasure.

The creative tension I have experienced between the spiritual world and natural world also tends to keep me down to earth. My recurring dream reflects a transparency which permits me the writer and you the reader to ponder the connections between soul, sexuality, spirit and nature.

My only recollection of feeling depressed had to do with terminating a relationship that was getting too intimate, given the circumstances. That empty feeling lasted for only a few weeks.

As you reflect on your own journey, is there an inner desire to make the most in personal growth for the remainder of your journey? How does the natural world connect with the spiritual in your journey? For all of us someone will eventually say the words: "Earth to earth, dust to dust and ashes to ashes" as a decisive goodbye statement. At this point in my journey I ask, is there a permanent component embedded within the larger Soul of the Universe that proclaims that all is not lost or wasted? As a child I repeated nightly the words of the child's prayer "If I should die before I wake, I pray the Lord my soul do take." What is the ongoing story of one's soul at the end of the journey on earth? Is there more than simply the eventual blending of my remains with the soil of the earth?

As you read these essays, some answers to these questions may come to you by reflecting on your own journey. Reflections illumined momentarily by whatever light radiates from my story. The pages of this book are intended to be a story and not an historical account in the usual sense of an autobiography. In an autobiography, research and accuracy impede the work of the soul.

This is a reflection on the journey of one soul, mine over the greater part of a lifetime. Reflection is an exercise without words. The task of putting into words the aesthetic sensibilities and the real essence of reflection on a life is an imponderable task. As I began to look back over seven decades of memories, use of the traditional historical time-frame method turned out to be a boring exercise. A soul time approach appears to be a better format for recounting my journey.

The format of my story then is not chronological data of historical events. Instead it is a reflection, a now back to then, account of the journey of my soul through eighty years. I had intended to include some historical time lines in order to assist you in understanding the impact of current events which helped to create the stuff of my soul. Those events certainly must have impacted decisions that I made along the way. Yet I found that a timeline would have to be in a sequential order. That did not fit the essence of my soul. Instead I will move from one cluster of events to another. For example one cluster will contain reflections on my experiences as a student. Another cluster will focus on my tendency to start new projects in living out my varied career. Another cluster will be true to the nakedness of my dream. Timewise, these clusters of reflections will not necessarily fit into any one period. Souls do not grow in the same time frame as physical or psychological stages of development. There is a maturing of the soul that comes from experience in maintaining a comfortable tension between spirit and nature. My reflections reveal that time, measured in years, is only one of several factors in attaining such maturity of the soul. When I retired as a counsellor one of my peers called me "a wise old pro". I trust that he had a glimpse of my soul, rather than speaking about my wisdom as a therapist.

It may well be that my soul does not stop growing with the announcement of "ashes to ashes and dust to dust."

Travelling along the road paved by a creative tension between the spiritual and natural world, I moved far beyond the indoctrination I received from the Primary and Shorter Catechisms of the Presbyterian background of my ancestors. The stark division between Good and Evil has been superseded by a healthy tension between the spiritual and the natural. On reflection, it appears that maintaining an appropriate balance in this tension, I was spared some dark nights of the soul. The brighter and more enlightened days of my soul were not accomplished by my own efforts alone. Parents, other family members, friends and co-workers played significant roles in the making of the stuff of my soul. In addition, when reflecting, I realize that certain of the enlightened days of my soul were pure gold, gifts of grace; meaning that neither I nor others did anything to warrant the gift.

To become entwined with the soul of nature requires reaching out in ways which are not easily available to those who live entirely in big cities. One has to experience the rawness and power of nature, like when caught in a major storm. Or like when the 7.0 magnitude earthquake hit San Francisco in 1989, I was walking along a street downtown in that city. Many of those who survived the tsunami of Boxing Day, 2004 in South East Asia will understand. Those who work closely with nature have a definite advantage in attaining a soul relationship with the Soul of the Universe.

I move back in time this morning as I watch the news of the tragedy in Northeast Japan. The live pictures on the screen bring on emotions arising out of reflection. I am back in San Francisco. I feel the connection of my soul with the soul of nature.

For the twenty years following my retirement I have worked growing Christmas trees. Not farming in the usual sense. Instead, I was working a clear-cut wooded area, nurturing the new growth of balsam fir trees which regenerated on their own. The exercise of growing trees has been good for my soul because I worked closely with the soul of nature and the Soul of the Universe. My respect for nature is merged with my own skills and understanding. I was able to work on the product of nature, a tree, and make it even more beautiful. I saw myself as a link in a chain of creativity including children and parents, as they decorated their trees for the celebration of Christmas. One amazing discovery has been that after selectively cutting the same area each season, there was always a new crop to be cut the following year. Nature did its part as I performed my creative work, and I believe that God blessed my cooperation with Him, in His role as Soul of the Universe. I believe that He smiles at the results.

Reflecting on my journey has taught me that my soul has been entwined with both the soul of nature (in the Irish theology sense), and with the Soul of the Universe; in other words, God, nature and me. The Soul of the Universe was there when I reached out, such as those times when I was in the little Church in Pemberton, British Columbia.

Note: The appendix entitled Chronological Order lists the events in the life of the author and provides an option for you the reader to choose the order in which you read these essays.

Searching For the Meaning of Soul

Several of the reflections that emerged into my awareness came as complete surprises as I contemplated my journey. Experiences and pictures from the recesses of my memory that were long since forgotten returned with new understanding. A few of them were gifts of grace which have been significant along my journey.

An event that is a gift of grace differs from all the other events. Each gift of grace has no connection with what I have done to earn it. For this reason I feel blessed. I believe that my soul has been involved with the Soul of the Universe in the process. A gift of grace is relative to, but not the same as, the special gifts received from friends or family. Gifts of grace are few over a life time. I did not expect the gift and I have not asked for it. Reflecting on my journey, I discover that the gift made an impact on my life.

Two of those gifts were the cause of turning points in my life. An individual may have been involved as the carrier, similar to a soul-like federal express. The source of the gift is always the Soul of the Universe. Why I have been selected is a mystery.

How different my life would have been had not the Soul of the Universe intervened when I was eighteen years old. Was John Ball my minister the medium? There was that one brief encounter in my Grandfather Reid's driveway, when John Ball asked me if I had thought of going into the ministry.

My soul friend relationship with a long time friend was neither expected nor earned. It just happened. There was no clear beginning and it is my expectation that it goes on into eternity. The ways and means that our souls use to make this happen are a mystery. This one gift of grace did not have any one moment of surprise. I reflect on this particular gift. It came gradually over the years, beginning with our first meeting.

A thing of beauty can be experienced as a gift of grace. I know of many influences that led to my decision to travel around the world upon my retirement. Other people were involved. I do not understand the power that led me to go out of my way in India to see the Taj Mahal. I did not know the story behind its creation. No one suggested that I make the train trip out of Delhi to see it. I just went, not expecting anything wonderful. As I experienced the beauty and read the story behind its creation I seemed to be responding to one of the great fundamental unchanging elements of the Soul of the Universe, *beauty*. Why did this experience have so great an effect on me? I believe that one of my soul friend relationships was involved. Those of you who know the story behind the Taj Mahal will understand.

There have been times when I experienced very special gifts that do not fit as gifts of grace. The close affinity of my soul with the soul of nature has given me several magic moments. I have stood in wonder at the complexity of nature. Frequently I have absorbed the beauty of nature. There have been moments as if I were standing on a pinnacle, selected by some unknown power to wonder at a particular scene: a sunset in a special place, a rainbow where one end pointed to the farm house where I was born. Yet no one of these events would fit into my category of grace.

The one element of grace in all of those experiences with nature is the following: the gift of grace in these instances is that my soul, the soul of nature, and the Soul of the Universe intertwine during the experience.

There have been occasions when I wondered at the beauty that is created when the soul of nature and the soul of man work together. My working with a self-seeded balsam fir tree to create a Christmas tree is one example. A thing of nature is made more beautiful by human hands. It is my understanding that a beautiful Christmas tree does not fit into the category of grace.

You the reader will have received your own gifts of grace in different ways. Reflect and be grateful when you arrive at your moment of surprise. Your soul will become more beautiful as a result. You and I can express our gratitude to the Soul of the Universe for those gifts. If you choose not to give credit to the Soul of the Universe then accept the advice of Thornton Wilder who said "My advice to you is not to inquire why or whither, but just enjoy your ice cream while it's on your plate."

My understanding of the concept of soul grew incrementally over the ten years of reflecting its meaning and function. I began with a concept I had learned from reading the book *Anam Cara* by John O'Donohue. There was little clarity in that Irish theology concept about the nature and functions of the soul. He did maintain that we are more than clay. He defined the nature of the soul from his experience of the ability of certain souls to connect with other souls to create soul friends.

During this journey I came to a much richer understanding of the soul. The concept of soul best describes for me that aspect of the person which ties the transcendent and the earthy and human together. In my understanding of the soul of nature and the natural world, I saw clearly that not only are we more than clay, but also we are more than mind. We are more than the five traditionally accepted senses, seeing, hearing, smelling, touching and tasting. I realize that my soul has had a two way functioning relationship with every one of these entities of my being. My soul functioned as a leader, posting signs along the journey, always leaving me the freedom to choose the way to travel. My soul has been the efficient and silent CEO working behind the scenes managing the input from other people, from the soul of nature and from the Soul of the Universe. My soul functioned as a mentor providing information and encouragement that resulted in improving the quality of my journey. My soul utilized various means to inform me and encourage me. The principle vehicle by which this service was provided was my relationship with other souls.

My reflections in the essay *My Soul Do Take* provided me with an assurance that all is not lost when someone pronounces those last parting words over my body "ashes to ashes and earth to earth." Although it remains a mystery as to how the separation will happen, I believe that my soul will enter an ongoing relationship with the Soul of the Universe. The one whom I have called God from the day I first repeated that childhood prayer.

My reward for a decade of reflecting on my journey is a greater sense of who I am at this juncture of my life. The tone of these essays will communicate the sense of satisfaction that I have gained about who I am; neither saintly nor murky, an ordinary soul who benefitted from widespread support and unexpected opportunities.

Before you tuck these essays away on your bookshelf, read again the recurring dream recorded in the introduction. Put the book aside and go to your favourite quiet place where you will not be interrupted. Give yourself time to reflect on whatever themes arise from some recurring dream. Your soul will be there to assist you. Reflection is an exercise without words. Surprises have a child-like way of becoming part of our journey. Your soul will want you to follow the wisdom of Thornton Wilder about enjoying you ice cream. The essay *The Meaning of Soul* emerged from my experiences when reflecting on a journey that covers eight decades.

It was only after formulating my own definition of soul that I researched the literature for definitions of soul. I have not joined the discourses of the theologians. It has not been my intention to begin a debate over any theologian's theory.

In our modern culture the word soul is used in the media in reference to people, corporations, and various forms of community. The media takes for granted that its viewers and readers understand the concept. The idea that the soul is part of an individual's makeup has been around for centuries. I studied theology at three theological schools, receiving degrees at each one. Not one of these universities provided me with any understanding of soul.

My reflections have provided certain images for which there appears to be no scientific including the psychological, answers. Reflecting on my journey in life, I have found that there are certain people with whom there develops a most meaningful relationship, and there is no way of explaining why it happens with some individuals and not with others. Young people explain this occurrence with the adage, "the chemistry is right." Is it possible that herein is one of the functions of the soul? Two souls connect in a manner which cannot be explained psychologically or physically. The how and why is a mystery.

In the book by John O'Donohue entitled *Anam Cara* the words "anam cara" mean soul friend. Reading this book many years ago was such a good experience that I kept going back to it. Reading it helped me to understand the concept 'soul friends'.

On reflection I remembered how the idea of soul was used in the Annisquam Community Church. Every Sunday the usher recorded the attendance on a chart that was posted in the vestibule of the Church. The heading on the chart was "Souls In Attendance Today."

As a child and through my teenage years my family talked about great uncle David, a retired Presbyterian clergyman, who had been influenced by spiritualists. He had lost two adopted children in death, and was led to believe that through a spiritualist medium he could communicate with his deceased children. I remember meeting him on an occasion when he visited his brother my grandfather Reid. Uncle David was on his way to a convention of spiritualists in Sweden. He returned from the conference with ghost like photographs of his children. The photographs were supposedly taken while he was in communication with the deceased children. I still believe that my uncle was being ripped off. He was vulnerable as a result of his loss. I know that he correctly believed that an important aspect of the person does not end with death. Uncle David was willing to be vulnerable in order to explore his belief that some sort of communication could take place between the living and the deceased. However his exploration led him into involvement with the occult. A better understanding of the soul, together with a willingness to accept the mysteries of the workings of the soul, might have prevented him

from getting involved with an occult group and
getting ripped off financially.

It seems that there are reasons why there has
been little exploration of the attributes and meaning
of the soul. Occult practices and radical
fundamentalist thinking are misguided attempts to
break through the mystery. My musings offered here
should not lend themselves to occult thinking. I
simply see these musings as a reflection of an
emerging understanding of what "soul" means to me.

Reflecting on my life from a soul perspective has
been a journey in itself. It has taken twelve years to
reach this point. I have arrived at a few conclusions
that have become part of my belief system. There are
conclusions that belong in the category of mysteries.
There are other ideas that are still in progress,
requiring more time for reflection and experience,
before they form part of my belief system.

Early in these reflections I came to understand
that the soul does not function through time in a
linear way as does the development of our physical
bodies. The soul operates and develops more in line
with the time frames of developmental psychology.
(Erikson etc.) This discovery led me to discard the
initial notion of recording my journey as an historical
autobiography.

The art of reflection with its tendency to surprise
is central to the ways of the soul.

The Meaning of Soul

*Soul is a term rarely used with precise definition in
philosophy, religion, or common life.*
Charles W. Ranson

Reflecting on my life journey as an exercise in
searching for the meaning of the idea of soul led me
to believe that soul is more than an idea. Soul is more
than a construct used to describe one of the mysteries
of life.

As a real entity soul describes the essence of a
person. Soul is different from and more than spirit,
mind, ego, heart (when used to signify compassion)
and the five senses. There is a two way interaction
between all these aspects of a person and the soul.
Also, there is a two way interaction between the
earthly and the soul.

The world of nature, of which the body is a part,
can be understood as having a soul. The family
system in which a person functions can be
understood as having its own soul. The soul of a
person is involved in a two way interaction with these
other souls over the course of a lifetime. The soul of
the individual person differs from these other souls.
Even the soul of nature may be vulnerable to
destruction by humankind but I believe that over
eons of time the Soul of the Universe would create a
new world of nature somewhere in the universe. The
human soul is more than these other souls in that it

continues on after a person dies. The soul which
describes the essence of a person is connected in some
mysterious way with the Soul of the Universe (God).
Most religions believe that the soul of a person and
the Soul of the Universe can meet in communion,
such as prayer and meditation.

The soul exercises various functions over the
lifetime of a person. For example it may influence
decisions and the choices a person makes at key
junctures of a life journey. The reverse also happens
in that the soul grows and matures as a result of its
interaction with these other souls: the soul of the
family, the soul of nature and the Soul of the
Universe.

This understanding of soul has emerged out of
my reflections on my journey that encompasses
eighty eight years. This definition of soul is still
emerging as I continue my journey. One example is a
growing belief that my soul has known before I knew
in my mind, which route I would take at specific
junctures along the way. I still had free choice, yet my
soul had a sense that I would choose one way and not
the other at the fork of the road. I would like to know
more about how that works.

In my situation the soul of nature made a
significant impact on my decisions. I do not have a
clear understanding of this function of the soul. In the
same way, gifts of grace that have come my way are a
mystery.

My search began from reading the book *Anam
Cara*. In his book *Anam Cara* John O'Donohue might

have provided more clarity on his understanding of soul friend relationships. Reflecting on my eight decades, there have been several such relationships. I have come to understand soul by examining those relationships. I identified two of them in another essay, J.J. Creighton and Don McLean. There were two others who stand out in my reflections.

The nature of those four relationships differed in each. Yet, they had one important quality in common. Each individual had a commitment to supporting the key aspect of my career: a ministry of assisting God in helping people to feel better. In each of the soul friend relationships the commitment involved hours and days of time together. Fulfilling their commitment was far beyond anything that I had expected.

Gifts of grace indeed! Their unique skills and their personal characteristics differed. The sameness of purpose was the one common dominator. J. J Creighton and I dug ditches together with pick and shovel in Nova Scotia. I learned about caring for one's own soul from one of those soul friends with her discipline of doing daily meditation. Another of those soul friends and I skied in British Columbia and roamed the meadows of Mount Rainier in Washington State. Don Maclean and I were together on car trips from Vancouver to Seattle to do volunteer work with the American Association of Pastoral Counsellors. These were but a few of the activities that cemented those soul friend relationships.

I sat on the chancel steps of West Vancouver United Church in June of 2010 with a group of children who were between the ages of three and ten years of age. I used a Christmas tree and a humming bird's nest that I had brought from Nova Scotia the day before, to illustrate my story about helping God. I encouraged the children to talk to their parents about how they could help God. Soul work was happening in that congregation. The responses of the children and the feedback from adults following the event confirmed that the souls of individuals, the soul of the gathered community and the Soul of the Universe were very much alive.

The common milieu for the emergence of soul friend relationships is that of assisting the Soul of the Universe in helping people to feel better. One example will illustrate. After a difficult meeting in the common room at the Training Centre in Tatamagouche I was alone in a large classroom. I was looking out the window and was crying. Out of the darkness a voice beside me said "It takes a big man to cry." That was the beginning of a soul friend relationship that continues to this day.

I have come to believe that the soul begins like a compressed bit of energy. A catholic medical doctor from Bogota told me she was taught that the soul is a tiny spark. She had no idea what that meant. Her mentors may have been on the right track. Yet, how could a tiny spark be big enough to contain the physical body within it, let alone be connected to the soul of the natural world? Thinking of soul as energy helped in my understanding.

This soul energy develops and grows as a result of the two way flow of energy between the soul and the five senses, the physical body, the spirit and the mind. This belief about a two way flow has made an impact on these essays about my journey. The soul that begins as a compressed bit of energy may develop into a beautiful or a murky soul. With change being one of the constants of the universe a soul can grow along the journey.

The concept of soul best describes for me that aspect of the person which ties the transcendent, the earthy and the human together. As John O'Donohue in his book reminds the reader, "we are from the clay. Yet we are more than clay." Also we are more than mind. We are more than the five traditionally accepted senses, seeing, hearing, smelling, touching and tasting.

Soul, spirit and ego are different ways of attempting to explain the individual person in other than materialistic terms. I prefer not to use each of these terms interchangeably. It will be from habits formed that I appear to switch from one to the other. Soul is simply a much better word because spirit is too limited in most peoples' perception. Spirit does not connect the human, the earthy side of the person and the transcendent. ('Transcendent' is used in the sense of the spiritual or metaphysical aspect of the larger universe). Spirit does not serve to connect our spiritual side with nature and the physical universe.

My experience as an earthy person, one who is close to nature, impels me to recognize the unity and the wholeness of the universe. The Buddhist tendency to equate the word God and the word Universe appeals to me. The universe being larger than anything we know about the physical world includes the transcendent.

Spirit belongs to the transcendent world and does not relate sufficiently to the whole person. A friend who was with her father when he died commented to other family members at the actual moment of death, "Dad's spirit is gone." She assumed as a medical doctor that there would still be some heartbeat, but that his spirit obviously had left his frail body. Soul would have been a better word than spirit.

Ego in Freudian terms is more of a scientific term and could be visualized as being at the other end of a continuum. Spirit is at one end and ego at the other. Ego is a psychological term that is open to scientific explanation. It is earthy but not transcendent. Ego is too much of an individual concept, which does not reach across or out to other souls. Ego does not reach out to a transcendent God nor to the larger aspect of the universe. I checked ego in a thesaurus and found there that both soul and spirit were incorrectly listed as synonyms of ego.

The book *Anam Cara* about soul friends, presents a picture of Celtic spirituality that avoids the dualistic concept of the universe where soul and human nature are direct opposites. My belief is that soul best describes the relationship between the human person and the Universe. In several religions this relationship is between the human person and God.

The soul as I understand it allows me to consider and accept the wholeness of life, including a life beyond death. There is no place or need in my thinking for the idea of a physical resurrection.

One aspect of the soul which appeals to me is the abundance of mystery surrounding the functions of the soul along the path of my own journey, and the observed journeys of other people. The mysterious has its own beauty. Real mystery cannot be explained. Trying to explain it takes from its beauty. I believe that many mysteries will remain just that, mysteries. That is part of their beauty.

There are aspects of my relationship with nature which are a mystery. Those times when nature appears to be closely connected with the transcendent are a mystery. I have been inspired by nature at times in ways which cannot be fully explained either physically or psychologically.

In *Anam Cara*, John O'Donohue offers the metaphor in which he describes the body as being in the soul. The medical doctor from Bogota was fascinated by O'Donohue's metaphor of the body being in the soul. This metaphor helps me in understanding that the soul is closely connected to a larger universe, that it is not limited to a small light somewhere inside my body. It makes it easier to take the next step of accepting that one soul can closely relate to and communicate with another soul. The how remains a mystery. The mystery is part of the beauty of life.

The soul concept is useful in accepting, without knowing, the mystery of how prayer and meditation are effective in so many different situations. I was present, but not directly involved in one particular instance where a small family group of friends gathered for a healing circle on behalf of the mother and wife in that family. The woman was critically ill in a hospital in a distant city. Their healing circle assisted in the immediate improvement of her condition. This experience has been replicated in several research projects. See Prayer is Good Medicine, by Larry Dorsey.

Where from and when my soul became mine are mysteries. Was it at first breath or at conception? Did the Soul of the Universe, at some point in my journey, share with me a spark of energy from His Soul?

How the soul communicates with other souls is also a total mystery. If there is a two way communication between my soul and God, that remains a mystery. I utilize e-mail and the Internet, without fully understanding how they work. Yet this new technology is not a mystery.

Where my soul goes at the time of my death is a mystery. One of my long held beliefs is affirmed by my recent discoveries is the following: meaningful aspects of intimate interpersonal relationships are much too beautiful and significant to be snuffed out like a candle at the time of death. Only an ironic and somewhat cruel God could create such a universe, in which the human person is granted the beauty of meaningful relationships, and then permits them to fall like a dead leaf from a tree. Reflecting on my journey strengthens this belief. Still the mystery remains.

During my years as a pastoral counsellor there were individuals who came to me for help who amazed me by the extent of their personal growth. At times an individual's growth was a mystery to me. There was nothing that I said or did as a counsellor that could explain the change. No particular theory of counselling could be credited with the change. Granted, my training as a therapist prevented me from getting in the way. Ego, psyche or spirit are of little help in explaining the personal growth of some individuals in therapy. It is plausible that certain attributes and functions of the soul, as outlined above effected the growth in a client.

I love mystery more and more as I grow older. Yet I am always on guard against trying to act unwisely when facing a mystery, as did my Great uncle David, a clergyman who got involved in a cult. I accept the mystery and move on rather than trying to explain why.

Some twelve years after the death of my father he let me know that my soul was connected with his soul. I was not consciously aware that it was his birthday. That particular one-time event is a mystery. It happened on his birthday. He died on his birthday and I was holding his hand at the time. Neither memory, nor ego, nor spirit can explain that mystery: it simply is. I was appreciating the beauty of a mountain in a brief break between counselling

sessions when the event took place. Could it be that
certain attributes of souls were involved in the
connection between mountains, the soul of a deceased
father and the soul of the living son? Were we
momentarily connected in a universe which of its
very nature is a unity? I accept the mystery as a
beautiful moment in my life.

Reflecting on eight decades of my life from a soul
perspective has led to these ideas about the meaning
and function of the soul. My definition of the
meaning and the functions of the soul is still
emerging as I continue my journey.

It is my hope that you will want to explore the
notion of soul friends as that concept illuminates your
own special relationships. Those among you who
desire to understand the meaning and the functions
of the soul will find your life enriched by reflecting on
your journey from a soul perspective. Examining
your soul friend relationships could be a useful
starting point.

A Soul Enriching Day

The summer solstice was but two days away. I arrived at the Atlantic Christian Training Centre in Tatamagouche Nova Scotia for an eight o'clock breakfast meeting, having driven from Musquodoboit. The sun was high in the Eastern sky. The weather gifted me with a fine beginning for the day. My expectations were not high.

In order to face the task ahead of me I knew from experience that I would require three or four hours to be alone, to meditate and go down memory lane. I would wander about on the property known as ACTC.

I had been invited to a two day annual meeting at the Centre. My involvement was to be interviewed by Don MacDougal with a focus on the Vision of the Centre at its start up in 1955.

My involvement with those beginnings began a year earlier, when Elton Davidge and I discovered the Bay Acres property. Don MacDougal's involvement began fifteen years after my time at the Centre, when he eventually became a staff member and later a member of the Board of Directors.

Four of us had a breakfast meeting in the board room to assist Don and I to think our way into the exercise with the annual meeting group. That meeting would be later in the afternoon. I discovered to my surprise the extent to which I was into feelings rather than thinking. The exchange at the breakfast meeting

between Don and I soon developed into a run
through of the early vision that I had for the Centre.
At times I was being nurtured not so much by
breakfast food as I was by swings between sad and
joyful feelings. I was not and still am not sure what
the sad feelings were about. They were showing, so to
speak, on my sleeve. I felt secure and safe in the
company of the other three. This feeling of security
when at the Centre had its early roots from my first
sight of the property.

I set out later that morning to explore the
property and the buildings with the intent of further
preparing myself for the interview with the group. I
intended to be alone with myself, the property,
buildings and the past. I found during those four
hours prior to lunch that my solitude was
occasionally interrupted by meeting up with current
staff members who were doing their work preparing
for the next group.

Ross MacDonald's son was busy manicuring the
lawns. Three teachers who were part of a two day
seminar were on a break from their session; the theme
of the seminar was working with hearing impaired
children and youth. Debbie Cameron, a seven year
board member from the local community was
gathering flowers from the garden. Two local young
women were changing the beds and preparing the
rooms for the incoming group.

My moments of solitude were broken
intermittently by visits from souls of the past, who
were important in the development of the Centre. I

had a sense that J. J. Creighton was walking with me. Former members of the staff, individual students and guests came out of the past and joined with my soul as I wandered. One moment, there would be only two of us in a one on one exchange. At another moment, there would be a host of souls joining me as a cloud of witnesses to my experience more than fifty years earlier.

In one instant my wife Lillian was there with me reminding me of her support in those early days. Our three children Graeme, Janelle and Larry were there cutting their teeth into childhood. It was a perfect setting for them in which they would begin their days in grade school. As we wandered about, I imagined what they were doing back in British Columbia, in the here and now. At other moments it seemed that several of us were wandering as a lonely cloud, exploring the changes that God and others had made to this sacred spot.

I walked the mile into the village on the trail that was once the railroad. In the here and now there were no trains to look out for, as there were on those earlier walks. I went as far as the newly developed old wharf that was rebuilt as a park under the guidance and supervision of my eldest grandson, Micah. That project happened in September 2008 when the men of the community were left to manage both home and work. It was a period when the Canadian Broadcasting Company came to Tatamagouche for the program *The Week The Women Went*. Micah's father was a six year old when we first walked the rails.

An overall theme developed during those four hours that carried on into the afternoon session. "Change in the context of permanence" best describes what I witnessed and experienced. The changes were full of surprises and grace. Grace best denotes the unexpected and unearned gifts from the Soul of the Universe.

The permanence of the soul of the Centre suddenly became clear as I sensed the aroma of the mock orange blossoms, and of the rhododendron tree, now three times the size it was when I first saw it fifty-five years earlier. The towering old locust trees in front of the Campbell house stand to affirm that permanence. As do the hundred and fifty year old remains of the wooden foundations of the shipyards along the French river that bounds the South East side of the property.

Then as I roamed the property, an awareness of permanence took me back to the roots nurtured by the first French settlers and later by the Huguenots who came to settle the area. I became aware of the continuing influence of the past on this sacred place. Soul development has its own way of breaching the distances caused by time. History tells us that there was once a log chapel that served as a spiritual meeting place for those French settlers who were whisked away during the expulsion of the Acadians. Were some of them in the here and now joining me and a host of other souls in an interdenominational tour, each one of us experiencing the beauty of creation now made more beautiful by human hands? Language now was no longer a barrier to our meeting.

We explored the old Campbell house now made magnificent by creative planners and craftsmen. I wonder if one or two of these ancient souls stopped in wonder and awe as we moved from spot to spot. If souls could reveal the expressions on faces, mouths would be open and eyes wide in amazement. I recall one dark night when a youth group was in residence for the weekend. The lads put small lights in balloons and floated them up among the locust trees. Their prank worked. The girls in the Campbell house panicked. The local minister, who visited with the group earlier in the evening, told one of his bloody ghost stories. (In the last essay of this series you can read about the author's claim that in the future life we may be able to recognize close soul friends by the essence of their souls rather than by other characteristics, such as a light in a balloon.)

An awareness of the changes that emerge over time came upon me as I studied the Norway spruce that were planted after my departure from the Centre in 1965. I assume that they were uprooted as seedlings from the hills of New Annan. One of those towering spruce now has a diameter at the stump of over two feet and a circumference of four or five feet. I sat and meditated on how many times the cells in my own body have split over the life of that tree. And how many more divisions I have before I lay me down to sleep for the last time. The day when I have finally used up my last division of cells, some malady overcomes my now weak immune system, and my soul joins the Soul of the Universe.

I sat for a time on the front steps of the Campbell house, reflecting on the purpose of this day. What was I doing, what was the annual meeting attempting to do, by way of a reflection on the past? A recurring image came to me. Once again I saw Chicken George of Haley's book, Roots, holding his young son on his lap telling him "Son you gotta know where you have been in order to know where you are going." I had no sense of longing to return to the past, simply yearning for the life expanding exercise of finding out where I am heading.

Mysteriously, the souls of two individuals appeared to me, one young Paul some 19 or 20 years into his journey, holding seventy two year Janie on his lap. Both were winter students. Janie was reflecting on her journey as a nurse, housewife, widow and sister of two elderly nurses. Paul was searching, not knowing that his journey would lead him into the ordained ministry, being married and divorced twice, remarrying his second wife, becoming the father of five children from his first marriage, and naming one of them after our daughter Janelle. I wondered as their souls joined me for these here and now moments; just how much of Janie's journey contributed to Paul's journey during those intimate moments. How many other exchanges such as that one impacted the lives of hundreds of individuals over the years since I first set eyes on this place? It is a mystery just how one soul in such an intimate exchange impacts the development of another soul and how much each person is moving on into new places and new directions. Souls seem to know more than I do about the direction and about the role of fate and grace during one's journey.

Arising from those verandah steps, my feet led me toward Stewart Hall. I saw a few persons moving about. I knew that the group was here for a two day seminar. They were having their morning coffee break. Entering the dining room, I observed that fifty teachers were seated at the round tables enjoying a drink, fruit or muffins. Noticing that I was an outsider, one of them invited me to sit with her group. She made room on a chair for me and I was welcomed not as an outsider but as another soul. They were eager to share of themselves.

Seated around those tables, they were a close knit group. They were part of a new but temporary community that had developed over two days. The historic tendency of the soul of this place was still at work. The soul of the Centre has a way of melding permanence with change.

Returning to my solitude I recalled the song in the musical "Tradition, Tradition, Tradition." I reflected on the tight boundaries of a close knit community that is in conflict with the eternal value of including newcomers. That old conflict was resolved in the here and now by the members of a group of six people who included me during their extended break.

Our encounter was meaningful and nurturing. It happened during the last hour and a half before their departure for their homes and families. I witnessed two of these teachers expressing goodbyes and sharing hugs as they went to their cars at noon.

On reflection I recalled the story of one individual who came back for a one time counselling session two weeks after he had attended a workshop at the Centre. He had been part of a week-long group. He arrived home expecting to be received and included by his family in the same spirit and manner of the group he had left. He was deeply troubled because in his words: "Even the dog did not take notice of me as I walked into my home." He left the counselling session with some awareness of how he could help his family to learn the value of including and opening doors for others. He saw a clear alternative to feeling sorry for himself.

Souls have their own means for making it possible for souls to connect and reconnect. On days like this one, souls from the past reconnect with my soul. Coming from the past they join me in the here and now to enrich my life as I continue on my journey. Two of those soul friends are now dead, yet their souls still influence my journey.

Is it possible that I have sufficient time and opportunity to become a soul mate with one of the new individuals whom I met on this special day at the Centre? I would welcome the opportunity and make room for him or her in my busy life. One requirement would be that we give each other space and time to reflect on our individual journeys. Souls do need plenty of room to grow and develop. Once again, there emerges the age old conflict of making room for values and people of the past.

I thought about some changes I saw that day in Tatamagouche. Where is the century old orchard sprayer that we hauled up from Waterville in the Annapolis Valley? It wouldn't have fit into Bob Latimer's archive room in Stewart Hall, but it could have been maintained as an historic relic on the grounds.

The physical changes in the chapel now provide a feeling and atmosphere of the new age movement. No longer does the chapel feel like a place where young teenagers would experience a deep sense of communion with others and with God. Something spiritual happened in those older experiences that was a surprise. Perhaps the architect, Keith Pickard, had a vision about spirituality without knowing how powerful its outcome would be. There was a sense of oneness and communion with the Soul of the Universe that these young people had not experienced in their Church back home. I remembered how back then, a trio from the session of one of the Churches in Truro came as a delegation to ask me to discontinue those services with their youth. Instead of learning from the young people, this session wanted to maintain the old. They were threatened by the new.

The chapel now has the feeling that the designers hope to assist the souls of modern youth to connect

with the Soul of the Universe with new age symbols. I
would rather see a merging of the permanence
together with new ideas and visions.

The Centre maintains and has developed its
original interest in building community to the extent
that this is one of its three bottom line missions today.
In the secular world of the twenty first century, new
symbols and rituals are needed to make room for the
Soul of the Universe to commune with those who
come to the Centre for renewal. Are there yet more
soul affirming rituals to be discovered by the Centre
that will enrich the souls of spiritual-hungry youth
and adults of tomorrow? To what extent can the
Centre learn from the past without returning to the
old rituals of another day? The new age rituals will
pass, yet much can be learned from trying to
understand their value and contribution to spiritual
growth. New images, new icons, are needed for the
chapel space. I have no concept emerging from my
soul for those icons. There are creative individuals
who can contribute to what might be. Will it be
Margaret or might it be one of the kitchen staff, will it
be Debbie because of her long experience at the
Centre? Whoever it will be, that individual will not be
alone in the new creation. Other creative souls will be
there. Possibly hovering around, one or more souls
from another realm who now understand better the
relationship between our souls and the Soul of the
Universe.

Using creative imagination can have a dark side.
Keith Pickard, an architect from Charlottetown, came

and lived with the students and staff in the old Campbell House for a week. We wanted him to get a sense of the purpose of the Centre before he set pen to the drawing board. He was with us in the midst of winter when the days were short and the sun set in the Southwest. Our error was in forgetting that the sun would set in the Northwest in July. The massive glass windows of the chapel face the Northwest. Today, six decades later, an architect would toy with ideas for storing the excessive heat that fills the chapel at the summer equinox.

The best vision will come from someone who knows and understands the roots of the Centre, yet who knows the importance of moving forward without reverting to what is mired in sentimentality. Yet I long for someone who will combine vision and imagination, who will come up with solutions and rituals that promote interaction between the Soul of the Universe and those souls who come to the Centre. The Centre operates in a very different culture today. I have been fortunate over my years to have a keen awareness of change. I am not uncomfortable with most changes to the Centre.

During the ten years from 1955 to 1965 souls from the past had an influence on my life without my understanding the meaning of soul. I was aware that there was a new depth to my spirituality that was related to the past history of the ACTC property. Comprehension of the meaning of soul is important for spiritual development.

Essay 5

Saints and Murky Souls

*Who shall ascend the hill of the Lord? He that hath
clean hands and a pure heart; who does not lift up
his soul unto vanity.*
                    A Psalm of David No. 24, E.S. Version.

A suggestion for your consideration; begin a
discussion with your friends about one of your
recurring peeves. How does your soul manage things
that annoy you?

Stand-up comedians Rick Mercer and Mary
Walsh are favourites of mine. I will cross the yard to
my neighbour's to enjoy their shows. It's good
entertainment. I have no desire to question the
accuracy of the message, nor do I attend Church
services to be a member of a captive audience,
entertained by a minister whose homiletical style is
that of a stand-up comedian. The medium becomes
the message. The wisdom of scriptural allegory and
teachings is blocked by the medium.

Out on my tree lot the messages that come from
the Soul of the Universe are not blocked by the
singing of a yellow warbler perched atop one of my
Christmas trees. I'm alone on the tree lot. The soul of
the gathered community is absent. I'll compensate for
the loss when I gather with friends and neighbours
after work to watch the final World Series game
between the Red Sox and the New York Yankees.
Another balance maintained along my journey.

Last evening I watched a three and a half hour program on the television. Millions of people from all over the world were with me watching the opening ceremonies of the 2010 Winter Olympics. There were no readings from the bible, nor any prayers to the Soul of the Universe. My soul suggests that I was witnessing a religious festival. There were mini sermons, K. D. Lang singing Hallelujah, a minute of silence in memory of a departed member, recognition of heroes of the past, and the final benediction with Wayne Gretzky passing the Olympic flame into the care of the cauldron set in the heart of Vancouver. Any pastor who watched the program and mulled over these similarities will have enjoyed the entertainment and the mental and spiritual stimulation.

I was present one Sunday when Peter Newbery conducted the service and preached the sermon as the supply minister at Mountain View United Church in Hazelton, British Columbia. Peter is a physician and minister. He is a member of the congregation. Peter conducts the service with dignity. Peter displays no need to compete with the comedian Rick Mercer. He holds his congregation at a "sit on the edge of your pew" attention. They hear a discourse relevant to the times and the personal situations of the worshipers. My words to Peter after the service; "I had to come over twelve hundred kilometers to worship in dignity and to listen to a great sermon. You gave us depth based on two allegories." One of those allegories was Ezekiel's vision of the bones in the desert. The other was the Gospel story of the raising of Lazarus. Peter's message was one of hope. My own spiritual journey within the structures of the Church has been influenced by the important personal ingredient of hope.

The minister of West Vancouver United Church is Ross Lockhart. Ross is a fine story teller. In his sermons he uses a story from the Bible on which to base his message. Last Sunday he used the story from the Book of Acts about Peter calling on a dead woman to get up and walk. In keeping with sound theology Ross tells us that the woman was in a coma. The message she heard from Peter was "Get up and walk. God has more for you to do." Ross reminds us that there are more opportunities for spiritual growth and service ahead. Saints believe that we can hope for better things down the road. Realistic hope has been a light on the path of my journey. I am open to accepting grace and mystery as part of the fuel mix that energizes me to travel the road.

My criticism of the leadership in the Church is grounded in my training. More so, it arises from the statistics which show that my own denomination has closed four hundred churches in the first ten years of the twenty first century. Six of those former congregations are in the rural areas surrounding Boiestown, New Brunswick.

Under the leadership of two of my physics professors at Dalhousie I studied the Gospels from a form criticism perspective. I slowly came up with a new tool which has been as useful to me on my journey as creative as man's discovery of fire for cooking. I became a creative critic. Like fire, skepticism and critical analysis sometimes lead one to skepticism. My soul has kept me from being a skeptic. Being a creative critic requires that I am open to the opinions of other people before coming to my own conclusion.

My reflecting leads me back in time to when I was about three years old sitting in the family pew with my Mom and Dad, my older sister Frances, and Seymour, a baby in Mom's arms. The pew was hard and for kids the service was long. An old man with a long white beard was quite visible in a seat that curved in such a way that a young lad could see him wondering if this was what God looked like. The choir consists of six or seven neighbours. The selection I remember as being a favourite is "In the Garden Alone." Critics before the days of gay marriages sometimes claimed that this hymn had a homosexual tone to it. If so then it may soon become an appropriate wedding march for gay Christians as they head for the altar.

It would be at the tender age of six when I started attending Sunday school. There was a small room, eight by ten feet, where one class gathered under the leadership of Mrs. Frank Kent. During the week I would have memorized five questions and answers from the Primary Catechism. There is no recollection of any interpretation of the answers. They were givens not to be questioned. Arriving in Sunday school and not being able to give the word for word

answer to a question from the catechism was a cause
for fear. With the question and answer period out of
the way we moved on to story time. Story time was a
valuable experience for me as a child. I learned more
from those great Bible stories than I did from any
catechism. I recall my fascination with the story of
Jonah in the belly of the whale and Daniel in the lion's
den. Was it because of our curious young minds that
our parents would read the story to us again at home?
They read from the King James Version. We knew no
other. The beauty of the language must have made an
impact on the mind of even a small child. What a joy
it would be if I could find an editor who could
transform this book into the beauty of that translation.
But who would read such; certainly not those
individuals who have been totally caught up in text
messaging shorthand.

When I return to that small room in the Riverside
Church in Musquodoboit, in reflection I pause to
ponder the images emerging out of another time.
Back then I was teaching younger Johns and
Margarets, some of whom were six years my junior. I
was only fifteen in grade eleven and was an obvious
candidate to replace the ageing Mrs. Kent. By that
time attendance had grown. There were more classes
in the little Church. A Sunday school superintendent
position comes up on the screen of my reflections. I
move into my first role of being the CEO of an NGO
(Non Governmental Organization). Such terms were
unfamiliar to me as I ordered supplies, looked after
the collection and coordinated the efforts of

volunteers in this miniature operation. My experience was somewhat similar to that of a university student going out into a cooperative experience. That small (enormous in my mind) experience at the time helped to pave the way for roads travelled through the years. My role as superintendent was only the first of several other leadership positions in those early years. Those experiences were the training ground for the responsibilities I assumed along my journey.

I have done my share as a volunteer in Non Governmental organizations. After retiring, I refused all requests to head up or even to work on committees. Now I could be my own boss. Now I would be responsible for managing the pressures of the market place. This new experience turned out to be much different than the pressures from committees, board members and volunteer treasurers. Instead of accepting requests to do volunteer work I would funnel some of the profits from the tree business into my favourite charities. Instead of making decisions that were influenced by board members I was now free to become part of a Christmas tree brotherhood sharing our experiences as tree farmers.

The Church has changed since those early days. It had to change in order to survive. Some of the change is obvious in the quality of the souls of ministers. As I reflect on the ministers who served in that congregation, several men and one woman come up. In my mind a number of them were saintly souls. The images of the men who have made an impact come

from points back in time. One is that of a Reverend
Reid. I would have been ten or twelve. The memory is
of a quiet very gentle man whose message spoke to a
young farm boy. Was it his gentle manner that made
an impression? Another minister I recall was the
Reverend Major Macintosh. By coincidence I had
dinner recently with one of his descendants. She and I
were guests in the same home on Bowen Island about
fifty years after his ministry at Riverside. Another
image is that of a large tall man whose speech and
manner fitted the image of a big man. It is the image
of Reverend Anderson. I assume that I have that
imprint on my mind because he died from a heart
attack while preaching his sermon. The impact of the
image does not come from remembering the actual
event, but through the reaction of the adults around
me. If I believed some of the Hellfire and Damnation
theology of the upsurge in current fundamentalism I
would conclude that he was being punished by God
for speaking the wrong words. That never entered my
mind.

Another clear image is of Reverend John Ball. His
influence on my choice of career at seventeen is
highlighted elsewhere. A red haired immigrant from
England by way of the Grenville Mission's work in
Newfoundland and Labrador whose pulpit style must
have been acceptable to this older teenager. I had
respect and admiration for him. In our home and in
the community he came across as a rough and ready
individual. I was aware that his table manners were
not up to the standards my parents taught me. His

appetite was that of a hearty farmer, who was not the least reticent about taking the last piece on the plate. I suspect that his rationale was that if he passed it by because of correct manners, a hungry worker would grab it anyway. Or maybe it was from a firm belief in the story of the loaves and fishes in the Bible. I had many meals in the Ball's home one winter and discovered that my suspicion that his wife was as good at cooking as she was at nursing was accurate.

I have worshipped in six different Churches where women were the ministers. We have a large percentage of female theological students in our seminaries. If there is hope for the future of the Church, there needs to be a balanced percentage of the female and male students in seminaries.

My first reaction to a woman minister took place in Musquodoboit. I felt a breath of fresh air as I listened to illustrations from the kitchen when she illuminated an important teaching from the scriptures.

Reflecting on eight separate women clergy, only four give me hope for the future of Christianity and the Church. The images of the other four are tainted with negative overexposure. Fifty percent success does not constitute superior leadership. Two of the women who get high marks served the same rural congregation in Nova Scotia. Fortunate indeed was that valley with two such ministries. The third woman minister worthy of a millennium scholarship had left a difficult marriage when she was already the assistant minister in a large city congregation. She was selected to be the new minister in a rural congregation. She brought compassion, understanding and an ability to communicate meaningful theological concepts to her flock. She is skilled in music, an added bonus for Musquodoboit, where the music department at the High school gets high marks. The fourth is one of two ministers at West Vancouver United Church. She is indeed a saint in her profession. I have worshipped under the leadership of the four ministers who come up with poor marks. They let their personal negative experiences consume how they minister to their congregation. Each of them talked about negative experiences with men. With one of them, the issues arose again and again, almost on a weekly basis. When I hear the song "where have all the flowers gone," I'm reminded about the disappearance of men in the Church.

Admittedly, gender has nothing to do with that fifty percent ratio between saints and murky souls in ministry. The results are more the consequence of poor initial screening. The pressures of political correctness prevailing at the time had been at the root of decisions to accept some candidates. Individuals serving on screening committees need to be more alert for candidates who are choosing the ministry as a career following bad experiences in life. Have the candidates worked through those experiences sufficiently to prevent the intrusion of the old baggage into their work? Will the seminaries teach them how and where to turn for support and help?

Effective counselling may help these aspiring professionals to separate their personal experiences from their work. Old problems can and do reassert themselves. Bad things do happen to good people. I believe that good men and women of the cloth should have worked through the bad things before they are accepted as candidates for training.

I recall negative experiences when worshiping under male leadership. Either the ministers have been boring and/or the sermon had lacked both depth and sound theology. One preacher I sit under occasionally is well trained theologically and his training shows. He appears to be guilty of two of the seven deadly sins namely, gluttony ad sloth. Attendance in that congregation is dwindling. Will it have to shut down in the near future?

I have never had a male preacher violate me by bringing to the service reports of his own bad sexual experiences. Such experiences have no place in the exercise of one's profession, whether ministry, therapy or growing Christmas trees. Reflection tells me that I have known fewer murky souls among Christmas tree growers than in the regular ministry of the Church. Training for the ministry of pastoral counselling involves considerable self reflection and thereby fewer murky souls.

The experience of reflecting on my journey from a soul perspective has been soul enriching. Memories of the saints who influenced my life are rich and numerous. I am not proud of the frequency with which memories of murky souls in the ministry of the

Church have surfaced. I sense that there is a link to my disappointment over the diminished influence of the Church in our secular culture. As for the murky souls, lessons learned; it is time to tie those memories to a balloon and let them flow upward, out of sight and away from the images imprinted on my mind. If my reflecting prompts you to follow suit then author and reader have connected as soul friends.

Interacting With the Soul of Nature

*Zen is the integration of the spiritual and the
mundane; an attempt to see the sacred in the
ordinary.*

Japanese essayist D. T. Suzuki

If you have opportunities to interact with the soul of
nature you are blessed. The nurturing of my own soul
and its relationship with the soul of the natural world
has been there from an early age. That relationship
has developed in close contact with nature. The essay
on my life as a farmer reflects the nature of that
relationship. It is only in the past two decades that my
understanding of the interaction between the two has
become clear.

My curiosity about the moon when I was but a
small child of four years of age is an indication of a
connection between my soul and nature. I noticed
that the moon followed us as we rode along in my
grandfather's car. I asked why the moon was
following us (everything else remained behind as we
passed them.) The lights were turned on within my
curious brain; it, soul and nature were in unison.

I'm writing within the context of a time when
there is great concern about the environment and
global warming, with the disappearance of animal
and plant species. Some of this concern is
demonstrated through public protests. I appreciate
those individuals who are activists on my behalf.

Those who protest are more effective when they understand the relationship between our souls and the soul of the natural world. My concern about global warming includes an appreciation of the Irish concept that animals and rocks have their own souls. There would be fewer disagreements among the scientists about the results of their scientific research if all of them understood that relationship. They too need to have a good understanding of the interaction between the spiritual and the natural world.

As a human being I have a unique place in the scheme of things. That uniqueness does not give me the right to dominate the entire natural world. To have received a God given right to dominate, as taught in the Shorter Catechism, was and is all wrong. Part of my uniqueness as a human being is in my responsibility to take what nature provides and with human hands and ingenuity to make it more useful and more beautiful. I have a responsibility for assisting the Soul of the Universe in maintaining a balance between the needs of the human soul and the soul of the natural world. I have listened to opponents to clear cutting in the logging industry. Not only were they unaware of our spiritual connection with nature, they had not done their homework. The result is harmful to the cause they promote. Likewise with some of those who protest against the seal hunt.

Those same protesters continue to contribute to the overpopulation of the world. There are those who protest against the use of any chemicals in the agriculture industry. I fault them for not doing their homework. Without the proper use of chemicals, their children could not be fed. Even as I write there is bloodshed in several countries, at the root of which is the scarcity of food. Many of the protesters live in buildings and park in car parks built on land where there was once fertile soil. The uninformed with good intentions are responsible for unnecessary delays in positive change. I am ever grateful to those protesters who do their research and homework.

The Halifax County Exhibition played an important role in the formation of my bond with nature. This agricultural fair was organized a little more than one hundred and twenty five years ago. As a lad I entered items to be judged. Prizes were given for collections of leaves from different plants, pressed flowers, seeds and insects. Long before the days of the 4H clubs, our teachers and parents helped us to collect, prepare and submit collections for the judging. Motivation was high and the lasting effect of being able to distinguish different species has been significant.

During my days on the farm and my years in the little one room school, incidents related to nature occurred that impacted my soul. I was exposed to roosters copulating with hens and a stallion breeding our mares. I witnessed dogs copulating and bulls mounting heifers in heat. When the stallion was called to the farm it was my task to hold the halter of the mare while the stallion mounted her. On another occasion it was my job to help steer the stallion's penis into the mare's vagina.

Together with my brother Seymour I snared rabbits by the dozens every winter. Quite often we skinned a rabbit and the meat was used for stew in our school lunch, kept hot at the side of the pot-bellied stove in our classroom. Or the rabbit was roasted together with dressing for the family dinner table. We trapped muskrats in order to sell the furs. We were adept at skinning the muskrats and curing the skins so as to get a good price. As I recall, our money was never wasted on things we did not need. We were taught to kill the rabbits and the muskrats with methods that did not cause them undue suffering. We thus learned respect for the soul of the animal.

My duties on the farm required that I learn how to neuter calves and piglets. With a sharp knife and a bowl of disinfectant I operated on many of these animals. It was part of the country culture and tradition. As I now understand all of this, I was working together with nature to maintain a proper balance in the order of things. During the years between fifteen and nineteen I slaughtered beef cattle and cows that were no longer producing milk. I slaughtered pigs, the meat of which was usually for family use. Occasionally I would take the whole processed pig to Archibald's store to help pay the bill for the family groceries. Over a period of three years I killed and plucked dozens of turkeys, using the most humane method known at the time for killing them.

We pierced the brain from the inside of the beak with a sharp instrument.

I recall my delight at being given the opportunity to take the dressed birds to Halifax and distributing them one by one to customers who had been lined up by my uncle Tim. He worked at the Federal Customs in the city. A larger order of turkeys was delivered to a grocery store located near the ferry in Dartmouth. It was exciting for this farm lad to have a ride on the old ferry over to Halifax.

My relationship with horses varied depending on the nature of the animal and the tasks at hand. During the period of my father's illness I was the one who made the kitchen fire when I got up, stoked the furnace and went to the barn before eating breakfast. In addition to feeding the animals one of my tasks was to curry the horses. In the winter one removed the horse blanket and gently tapped the horse encouraging it to stand to one side of the stall to make room for currying. I would brush the animal from head to foot with the curry brush.

After brushing the tail I would braid it and fold the braided hair up into a neat knob. On occasions over the years I drove the horses, usually as a team to the blacksmith shop for replacing and refitting the shoes. If my grandfather Reid's shop in Elmsvale was not open I would go on another five miles to Middle Musquodoboit. In between those times a horseshoe would come loose and I would lift the horse's heavy leg, hold the foot between my knees, pare the hoof and nail the shoe back into its rightful location. A certain skill was necessary so that the nail would come out up the side of the hoof for clenching so as to secure the shoe. It was important to drive the nail in the proper way so that it did not turn inward and enter the quick of the foot. Not only did I not want to hurt the horse, I needed to protect myself from the horse's response to a nail being driven into raw flesh.

On one occasion a frustrated and angry horse turned on me because the logs it was dragging were hitting against its heels. It was icy and on a downhill slope. I had to climb a tree in order to save myself from the wrath of the horse. The horse and I made up back at the barn. That was only after the logs had broken free and the horse galloped home on its own and into its stall.

As a lad, I decided to order bees and begin beekeeping. My parents insisted that this was not a good idea and my father made me cancel the order. Like many a soul, one day many years later I realized an ambition denied. I kept three hives of bees for several years. In total I produced more than a thousand pounds of honey.

Many years later while riding a bicycle on the sea wall of Stanley Park in Vancouver I thought to myself "my Dad cannot stop me now". Dad did not allow me to get a bike because he claimed that it was not good for me. Exercise was to be had by doing useful work. Even to this day I have to be most intentional about exercising my body by simply walking. I should be producing instead.

My relationship with the plant world began at an early age. I remember ordering seeds selected from a catalogue. They would arrive in our roadside mail box weeks later. I became a business man and sold some of the seeds at a profit. I planted tomato seeds and grew them in boxes and pots and later transplanted the seedlings to the garden. This began as a young lad before I reached ten years of age.

As I got older my farming tasks and skills increased in tandem. I remember plowing an acre a day with a team of horses using a single furrowed plough. I recall being taught how to make a straight furrow by keeping one's eye between the horses, focused on a selected point at the other side of the field. I was taught not to look back, or else the furrow would not be straight.

That admonition was very much the opposite of my advice to many clients in counselling. I would advise my client "Please heed the advice of Chicken George in Arthur Haley's book, Roots." Holding his son on his knee Chicken George advises him to look back on his heritage so that he can move wisely into the future. I have taken this admonition from Chicken George seriously.

A visit to see the renowned Golden Sitka Spruce on the banks of the Yakoun River on the Queen Charlotte Islands made a strong impact on my soul. My son Graeme and I drove on a woods road to the sacred home of the tree. That visit added a spiritual touch to my long time relationship with trees. Up until then trees were for firewood or to be made into lumber for building houses.

Cutting wild trees for Christmas trees in our pasture with my Dad when I was a child, had already taken on a wee bit of magic. Many years later, when involved in a project for my retirement, my soul presented me with a choice. That choice was between raising bees or growing Christmas trees. My soul sensed more magic in growing trees. There is magic in the celebration of the birth of Christ, with a tree in the corner of the living room. Christians borrowed the Christmas tree idea from pagan celebrations, representing new life and growth. Soul magic was ready at hand for this new aspect of my life.

In another essay I have written about experiencing the rawness and power of nature. I remember being in the midst of a large field when caught in a major blizzard. I had been assisting a family who were struggling to get their car moving out of a snow bank. If I could remain upright against the force of the winds blowing off Tatamagouche Bay I would survive. I barely made it to the shelter of the Training Centre. I was present for the 7.0 magnitude earthquake that hit San Francisco in 1989. I was walking along a street downtown Francisco when it happened. Surviving those experiences has helped in blending my soul with the soul of Nature. Many of those individuals who survived the tsunami of Boxing Day, 2004 in South East Asia will understand. In spite of all the destruction and death, those souls who work closely with nature have a definite advantage in attaining a soul-like relationship with the Soul of the Universe.

As I have benefitted from writing this journey of my soul it is my hope that my readers will gain from their own reflections as they ponder my thoughts and experience. The advice of Chicken George to his young son works like magic. "If you are gonna know where you are going you have to know where you have been."

Soul and Play

God wants to see more love and play in your eyes.
For that is your greatest witness to Him.
  Hafiz, 14th century Persian poet and Sufi saint

The wisdom of the quote above in its exhortation to love and play emphasizes one of the three parts of a definition of good mental health. A mentally healthy person is one who has a balance among the activities of working, socializing and playing.

Have you contributed to the balance in your life through reflecting on your soul's influence on the pleasure in your life?

Nearly a whole year has gone by since I walked and played in New Zealand for a whole month. That experience was a playful experience, high on the scale of my enjoyments.

Planning a trip and driving across the width of North America recently was exciting and could be considered a form of sedentary play. Sitting in an old 1992 Honda Civic for six days does not mirror my traditional ways of playing. It was the challenge that attracted me. The challenge of that drive at my senior age was food for the soul. I enjoyed the companionship with Janice who helped me drive from Fredericton, New Brunswick to Golden in British Columbia. We became soul friends over the time of the trip. We listened to great music on CDs. We shared memories of life in Boiestown. There was a lot of catching up for me since Janice was only a little girl when we left Boiestown; her Dad Gerald O'Donnell was remembered with fondness as I recaptured the past.

I'm looking forward to our second nuclear family reunion in Nova Scotia this coming summer. If the logistics are well planned and the program is kept sufficiently open this family time has the potential for achieving the status of becoming one of the highlights along my journey.

There is growing excitement within my soul as the time approaches when I will be the tour guide for a young doctor whom I met on one occasion a few years ago. She is planning to come to Nova Scotia on her vacation and wants to reconnect to discover whether our souls have the potential for becoming soul friends. Angela has spent some time in Vancouver and Calgary. She has lived most of her life in that massive collection of people in and around Bogota, Colombia. A couple of days working and roaming among my Christmas trees will be a new experience for her. Driving the roads and sharing the people and sights of the Maritime Provinces should be a playful experience. This could be a joy to remember. PS. I had the fun of planning and dreaming about this experience. Unfortunately it did not materialize.

Over the time since I was seven or eight years of age, through my ministry at the Atlantic Christian Training Centre, a pattern of play developed. Fishing and hunting with occasionally experiencing the

rhythm of the dip, dip and swing in a canoe form the
pattern. There was my soul's desire to play with the
soul of nature. My eldest son Graeme and his two
sons have inherited the pattern. A portion of my joy
has been in sharing play with the soul of nature
together with someone who has never had these
experiences.

In my younger days in Musquodoboit I fished the
Benvie, Kent and School House brooks. I learned how
to gig sea trout as they rested in a cool pool at the side
of the Musquodoboit River. I envied the skills of the
fly fishermen who could catch those elusive trout
legally. Our neighbour, Clary Muir, was a target of
my envy. My luck with a silver doctor fly was close to
zero. I reach back into my memory and can still feel
the struggling three pound sea trout that I caught
with my bare hands. It was marooned in a pool where
the Benvie brook ran under the railroad.

During my seven years of University and post
Graduate studies, fishing took a back seat. Then we
arrived in the heart of New Brunswick and I was
introduced to fishing for salmon and trout on three
major rivers in the central part of the province, the
Miramichi, Saint John and Nashwaaksis rivers.
Playing a twelve pound Atlantic salmon in the
Miramichi is a thrill to be relived only in memory.
The twelve-pounder was my only big salmon catch
with a fly rod. Climbing up the banks of the
Miramichi behind the parsonage lugging a wash tub
half full of sea trout temporarily earned me the title of
the best fisherman who ever set a rod on the river.

There being no limits on the size of catch, I could openly brag about my success.

Fishing with Sam Haines in a brook in Southern New Hampshire is easy to recall. It was our first such trip together. I had my first drink of cold beer with Sam Haines. Sitting on a log with the sound of the gurgling brook enveloping us, a drink of cold beer while enjoying lunch and the warmth of the sun still stirs up the temperature of my memory. A drink of beer became a new element in my playing. Sam Haines lived in Annisquam during the summers. He was a renowned physician at the Mayo Clinic in Rochester, Minnesota. In my eyes he was an old pro who was wise about the ways of life. He introduced me to the delicacy of a can of beer with my sandwich. Play with him provided food for thought and for my soul.

My deer hunting days began with shooting a deer in our orchard when I was only fourteen. Dad had an old twelve gauge shot gun. I wonder if that gun was the same one he used to shoot the only moose I ever helped to carry out of the woods. There were very few moose even in those days in that part of Nova Scotia. In my very younger days seeing a deer in the wild would be something like my first sight of an airplane flying over the valley. During my teenage years the white tailed deer increased incrementally in the area. There was no competition from hunters who came from the city in those days.

In the absence of hunters, deer became so plentiful that they were a problem. They ate from the family vegetable garden and trashed parts of the grain field. Hunting deer with a light became a new way to play, opening up an opportunity to share the fun with friends like Fulton Andrews. There were some risks involved in this pastime, but never a crisis. My brother Seymour and I never confessed to my uncle Eben Benvie that we may have been the culprits who put a bullet through the neck of one of his horses. It was a minor wound, so there was little need to confess. My enjoyment of hunting deer is now confined to my memories and my photographs.

I can recall with fond memories hunting on a Saturday with a fellow student Eldon Gunn when we lived together at Pine Hill. Hunting deer when living in Boiestown and Nashwaaksis was always one part of the balance between work and play. A single day hunt or the occasional overnight hunting trip usually included a companion hunter. The social aspect, eating lunch and developing a hunting strategy, were more important than bagging the deer.

I recall hunting alone one day after we moved to Tatamagouche. The particular day was not a success. The day did produce an experience of joyful laughter for me, out there alone in the woods. Hunting was poor because it began to rain. As I made my way along an old woods road I spotted the top of a glass jar protruding up through the fallen leaves; like a daffodil up through old grass. The jar was full of a clear liquid. Prior experience informed my curiosity that it was gasoline, left there by a logger a few years previously. The contents did not smell like gasoline. I decided to perform a playful experiment to prove my assumption. I found some dry twigs on an old pine tree and started a little fire beside a rock on the road. Everything was soaked with rain so there was no danger of creating a crisis with my strategy. I placed the bottle a few feet from the fire and walked back the road a safe distance with rifle in hand. With my 300 savage braced to my right shoulder I aimed at the jar and pulled the trigger. The explosion from the gasoline was greater than I had anticipated. I laughed and laughed with joy over the explosion. Suddenly I remembered that I had put my glasses on the rock by the bottle of gas. Only the lenses survived. The next evening I discovered that I could see the stars without my glasses. It was several years before I went again for eye tests and resumed wearing glasses. When I did give in to wearing glasses again I realized that for five years I had been missing the beauty of the stars far off in the heavens. Even today I seldom wear glasses for distance sight. A new pair will be needed following cataract surgery. Though my soul has grown more beautiful over the years, my vision has not kept up. Nature's intent may be to keep me humble.

Hunting rabbits with our two boys while we were in Tatamagouche was play. From the time of my early days in Greenwood school I learned how to make snares and place them in the rabbit paths in the woods. Hunting rabbits all through those early years was more of a business than playing with the soul of nature. Having learned the skill of archery while

living in Boiestown and Nashwaaksis, Graeme and I
decided to try our luck bagging rabbits with the bow
and arrow. We had a bit of luck but the catch was
minimal. Graeme, Larry and I shot and snared
enough rabbits to provide some pin money for the
boys. The price for a pair of rabbits had increased a
hundredfold over the years. Newfoundlanders living
in Halifax were willing to pay big money for rabbits
at Christmas time.

My very first experience with canoeing was very
embarrassing. While at Dalhousie University in
Halifax I was selected to be a delegate at the national
convention of the Student Christian Movement. The
meetings were at Lake Couchiching in Ontario. One
of the delegates caught my attention and fancy.
Marion was the daughter of Canadian missionaries in
China. Marion was a graceful and understanding date
and we enjoyed our time on the lake. It was my first
time in a canoe and my paddling skills were dismal.
The canoe insisted on going in circles until Marion
gave me my first lesson in paddling. Following up on
the experience I honed up both my dating and
paddling skills.

Two of the boundaries of the Atlantic Christian
Training Centre hugged the water. The Southeast end
of the property was defined by the French River and
the Northeast by Tatamagouche Bay. Part of the
magic of that paradise for me has been the association
with canoeing. George MacLean's father presented
me with my first canoe one summer in the late fifties.
I took to the canoe in a way like a duck takes to

water. There is something magical about paddling a canoe.

My previous experiences with canoes were on the Miramichi, Nashwaaksis and Saint John rivers when fishing for salmon and trout. One soon learns that paddling a canoe alone is an art that is executed differently than paddling with another person. One's rhythm must merge with the rhythm of another person. It is not unlike the rhythm necessary in the making of soul friends. During most of my canoe experiences on the Miramichi we used poles. Poling a canoe from a standing position is more of a challenge than an art. The force of the swift water served as the power. The pole was used to steer the canoe into a selected run of water or to snub the canoe in its tracks while the current pushes the canoe aside to avoid disaster when threatened by boulders. Where there was no current to act as power, one shifts gear and engages human power using the pole as a drive shaft. There is a stretch of water on the upper Miramichi appropriately named "Push and be Damned."

Canoes were never part of my early family life either on my mother's or father's side. Family history informs me that there was a canoe tragedy in the mid-nineteenth century that claimed the lives of three men on mother's side of the family. Canoes, like bicycles, were considered to be dangerous. Their legacy to my family was a fear of canoes. There are hopes that this inter-generational fear will not hinder my plan to include canoeing as part of our family reunions.

In my retirement, I was longing for a closer connection with nature by way of the canoe. I arranged play time to include day trips with a few of my soul friends. These day trips took me back to the Miramichi and St. John rivers. I recall two trips on the Musquodoboit river. The big plus on the Musquodoboit River was the magical connection with the past as I shared remembered childhood experiences with soul friends. Added to the serene atmosphere were the memories that automatically booted up as we slid by a particular land mark. A wild apple tree dressed in pink and white blossoms smiled at us as we sat on the bank of the river enjoying our lunch. Vestiges of the old railroad remain between the river and the highway. How many times would I have passed by that spot on the highway when walking to and from evenings to enjoy the company of my very first soul friend, my cousin Mary?

Nova Scotia, with its abundance of lakes, is an ideal area for canoeing. Lillian and I canoed on our honeymoon at Long Lake near Moose River, the site of the mining tragedy in 1936. In 2004 I canoed on Ship Harbour Lake and portaged over to another Long Lake; the same lake that claimed the lives of three of my mother's ancestors a century and a half ago.

The playful side of my soul was in full bloom when a soul friend and I stayed at Salmon River Lake for a short holiday. It was a time of relaxing, reading to one another, enriching our immune systems and exploring the area. Canoeing on the lake and swimming in the nude served to tie us closely to the water. One night we chose to sleep out under the stars in our sleeping bags. Mother Nature was a bit shy and decided to cover the brightness of the heavens with a brief cover of clouds. Rain began to break the stillness as the drops hit the leaves. On consultation we decided to pull up our bags to shelter our faces, and weather out the shower rather than disturb the magic moment by returning to the cabin.

It requires very little effort to listen again and hear the rain on the leaves above us while canoeing on another lake. We were paddling along when a summer shower appeared suddenly out of the blue sky. Huge maple trees had reached out over the water from the nearby banks. Years later I can easily regain the magic of those minutes waiting for the rain cloud to move on. The combination of listening to the rain on the leaves and watching the splashes as the large drops of rain hit the surface of the lake came together to create a sense of being merged with the soul of nature.

It was on that same holiday that we went exploring one day after an old-timer told us about a unique spot deep in the woods in the region. We followed his directions, and after an hour found the magic spot. Going through the gate and entering the compound, we were welcomed inside. The large cabin reminded me of pictures I had seen of homes in Scandinavia. We found ourselves in a different world. For a time we were in Sweden, not on the shore of a lake in the woods of Nova Scotia. Moving down the slope toward the water we found a Japanese tea house for our meditation. A couple of years later we returned to that spot one last time. The buildings were vacant this time but the absence of people only increased the enchantment of the place. We realized anew that what nature has created with all its beauty can in certain instances be made more beautiful by human hands. There is a drive within the human soul to return one more time to the scene of intense experiences. We had remembered the secret entrance to the tea house. As we meditated inside we thought about that creative family who developed this place, who imported images from Sweden and Japan. The soul of that family built their reflected memories into their Nova Scotia summer home. They infused that spirit into the buildings and made them integral parts of the landscape.

I grew up on a farm in the country where the blending of soul with the soul of nature involved work as much if not more than play. Even swimming was a form of cleanliness. There were other play times not connected with nature. Although attending Church had its boredom for children, we still played Church in the attic of my grandfather Reid's wood house. My playmates included my sister Frances and my mother's youngest sisters Kathleen and Olive. We played school up there as well. A makeshift pulpit and chairs for our pews and desks formed the setting for our games. We did not need a carpenter to build our movie sets.

Box socials in the mind of a fifteen year old lad were not associated with raising money for the temperance hall. A youthful and playful soul created mental images for the young men who were influenced by hormones at work within. One had to earn enough money working on the road, trapping musk rats or snaring rabbits to be able to be the successful bidder for a young woman's basket. Beautiful crafted boxes extracted higher bids. For some older men, fantasies about the home cooked goodies in the box motivated them to bid higher. It was more the hormonal activity for me. The prime motivation for me was getting either Rena or Blanche Andrews' box. If the owner of a box wanted you as a lunch partner then the secret was leaked to you in advance. The cagey girls who wanted to get the highest bid of the night leaked the secret to more than one unsuspecting bidder. I reflect on how I played the game by getting a friend to do my bidding for me. The auctioneer overlooked the subtle form of bargaining. And Blanche would have been relieved to discover that her admirer was John and not Jim.

At Sunday school picnics the three legged races, the tug of war and the associated prizes were fun. Rope swings were hung from the branches of large trees beside the Church. I was challenged to get on the swing. I always regretted having accepted the challenge. On reflecting I can still get that same feeling that my stomach would be wrenched from me as the swing reversed from the top of its rhythm to begin the descent. Was the fear of falling when I was a baby still with me? That fear has disappeared over the years. My family still objects to my going on the scream machine near Tampa in Florida. I love the thrills. For a much tamer ride, my cousin Susan and I have a ride on the horses of the merry go round at the annual Halifax County exhibition. Being kids again is great play.

In the Spring, Summer and Fall seasons there were occasional straw rides on farm trucks. The roar of a motor replaced the sound of the sleigh bells of a winter's ride. Carbon monoxide filled the air instead of the smell of horses breaking wind as they trotted along. These rides started out from the Temperance Hall where my trailer now stands as my Nova Scotia home. I recall two such rides to Clam Harbour beach. There was lots of anticipation and excitement about going to play in the sand and the rolling waves. I do not recall any fantasies about being with any one special girl. Another ride on the back of a farm truck with straw for cushions was when the Elmsvale Division of the Sons of Temperance returned a visit from a Division in Upper Stewiacke. I don't remember whether Abe Flemming was on board having had his customary nip at the bottle to make him more at ease in the social situation. If he were, he would have barely been able to stand up at the temperance meeting, placing his hand over his heart and repeating "worthy patriarch I have not."

My reflection of my playful soul prior to the earliest events recorded here stirs up warm feelings surrounded by events that I do not remember. There were reports that my mother's first pregnancy ended in a miscarriage. Reflecting on stories about her loss, I believe that she filled the darkness in her soul with attention given to me. My mother and older members among my relatives told me about the quality of her bonding to me. My soul has a quality about it that reflects her care and love. One of those stories records that she went down to the Boston States to visit relatives. I was not old enough to remember that she carried me along. No doubt it was my first train ride. All of that warm feeling centred on those early days with my mother has come by way of two sources of information: the cells of my body did not want to forget my mother's bonding with me and the stories that were told to me. As a child I did not make any connection between my mother's love for me and those events in her life. Eight decades later I understand how those events and her love for me were part of the growth of my soul. In turn, there was a secondary gain in her life because of the balance provided by the interaction between my mother and me.

A balance of interaction with other people, pleasure and work are components which form a triad that is essential for good mental health. Family responsibilities that began at an early age when my mother's mother died, leaving ten children, created an imbalance for most of her life. Reflecting on my own journey has provided a portrait of a balanced life; leaning toward the work portion of the triad.

Reflection is a tool available to humans for checking the balance between the three components of a healthy mental life: social interaction, work and pleasure. The soul is the chief executive officer that helps us in maintaining the balance.

Humour is Good For the Soul

If I had no sense of humour I would long ago have committed suicide.
Mahatma Gandhi

How you experience humour will depend in part on your cultural background. Your soul, in consort with that background, will influence your response to this essay. It is my hope that in reading these stories you will set them aside and reflect on your soul and humour.

Spontaneous humour is a factor in building community when a number of associates and peers get together. Ministers from the three Atlantic Provinces and Bermuda gathered annually in Sackville New Brunswick. Some of my funniest stories came from those meetings. Occasionally a story had a sexual component that would have no place at the pulpit. A Newfoundlander would tell a story about his own Newfie culture. Newfoundlanders are experts at laughing at themselves. The soul of the Newfoundland culture is unique.

Over my eight decades I have experienced real delight when I witness comic events in nature. I recall with ease the picture of a spotted baby deer bouncing two and fro wanting to play. It performed in a dance about twenty feet from me while I was on my knees butt-pruning Christmas trees. When its mother called it away the little deer ran some one hundred feet and peered out from behind a small tree. I wondered mischievously how the deer was solving a problem created by the conflict between its own and its mother's sense of trust.

I have laughed at the surprise experienced by a baby kitten while playing. Unexpectedly tumbling end over end was a brand new experience for it.

The Soul of the Universe communicates His sense of humour in a variety of ways. At times that humour has an ironic twist to it. As a compassionate and loving God his humour is never at the expense of other souls.

I know several fun stories about human souls appearing before Saint Peter at the pearly gates. Those stories are different from the humorous situations that I have witnessed in the world of nature. They are fiction, provided for entertainment, at times at the expense of other persons.

Reflecting on my journey covering the past eight decades, humour was related to sunny days of my soul. I have recorded in another essay how there have been very few times over the years when the dark nights of the soul have clouded my life.

When I reflect on the funny events and tales that stand out in my memory, I experience some of that same delight that I felt years ago. On occasion I burst out laughing, sitting alone while meditating on a reflected moment. My soul has been enriched by recalling those events and circumstances.

Responses to humorous events and tales appear to be related to the eye of the beholder. A group response to a funny story may have been ignited when one or two people found that it touched their funny bone. Others laugh because of their need to be included. I have been in a room with a group when I was the single person who saw no humour in the story being told by the stand-up comedian.

I recall how I felt like a stranger among British friends at a concert at the West Vancouver United Church. We had recently moved there from Annisquam, Massachusetts. Two men with a British background were demonstrating a humorous situation when two deaf persons attempted to communicate.

The depth and height of my delight in hearing or experiencing a humorous event changed from time to time. My sense of humour has changed in tandem with the growth of my soul. On reflection the differences appear to be related to the developmental stages of my life.

I checked Erik Erikson's social-psychological stages of development. My response to humorous situations when I was in my mid-teens differs from those when I was in my mid-fifties. My youngest grandchild at three takes great delight in situations that appear funny to him. His responses arise in face to face situations with another person.

There are two stories that stand out when I reflect back to the pre-school stage of my development. They were told to me by adults. My uncle Wellwood who had a hearing problem would use a bullhorn with the small end pointed to his ear to hear the response to his favourite story. I remember hearing one story at a very early age.

Friends of his father had joined the family at dinner. Uncle Well, as we knew him, would paint a picture of the visitor who had a mustache and a hearty voice. His description of the visitor's wife went like this. "She was beautiful with her red hair tied in a bob like the horse's tail. She wore a fancy white dress. There was so little dress above the table that I did not dare look under the table." It is easy for me years later to recall the enjoyment that showed on uncle Well's face as he delivered the punch line. Deep reflection really is an exercise without words.

The one other story that I remember from my early childhood was told by my Dad. I assume that it was second hand yet I have never heard the story from anyone else. It may have been a part of the folklore of the Musquodoboit Valley. The story was about a respected elder who lived on a farm five miles from Upper Musquodoboit, out on the Sheet Harbour Road. One August day Elder Flemming was hoeing his potato patch, which bordered on the gravel road. Two dudes from the city of Halifax were driving by in their horse drawn buggy, before the days of the automobile. They stopped to inquire of farmer Flemming about their location. They did not have the advantage of GPS. One of the city lads got out of the buggy, went to the fence by the ditch and called Mr. Flemming to come over. When they were face to face with the fence between them the visitor inquired "Old man, where does this road go?" The response "Well I have lived here nigh onto seventy years and it has not gone anywhere yet." Somewhat taken aback, the city-traveller expressed his disdain with "There is not much between you and a damn fool." To which farmer Flemming responded "Nope, just that fence."

My soul may have been influenced by the ironic twist in that story. I have a tendency of taking a word out of a serious exchange in communication and converting the wording into something humorous, thus distorting the meaning. Always being careful to avoid laughing at anyone, but creating a situation where we laugh together. If I have to explain the new meaning then the fun is lost.

Amusing pranks provided delight as I entered my young adult stage. Such pranks tended to be at the expense of others. Dr. Ian MacKinnon taught Church history at Pine Hill Divinity School. We liked him as a person more than as a well informed professor. He gave me my first lesson in skiing. With the help of an engineering student we attached a loud speaker to the phone system. A group of his students assembled in the common room of the residence to have some fun. One of us called Dr. MacKinnon at his residence number. "Is your house on the street car line?" Wanting to be of help he gave a positive response. The caller advised, "Don't you think that you had better remove it. There is a street car coming."

On reflection I discovered that certain humorous stories rang a bell for me as they applied to ageing. Two such stories came to the surface and are recounted in this essay. If told by a teenager still in the identity stage he would be making fun at the expense of his elders. When the same story comes from the mouth of a wise old pro it can be pure humour in the context of wisdom.

My soul and humour are closely connected .The two change and develop in tandem. Every soul is unique. The person sitting beside me will be laughing hysterically when listening to a story while I see or hear no humour. My enjoyment will be listening to and watching the other person lose control. I experienced such a situation recently when my grandson's wife was recounting a funny event. It took her some three or four minutes to regain control so she could finish the story.

I delight in retelling two events that involved me. Here is one picture as I retrieve it from the recesses of my mind.

I recall a situation in a classroom at the Atlantic Christian Training Centre. I was in my fourth decade. Several times a year I led groups of young people who came from their local Churches for a week end. Some of the sessions provided these young people with their first formal education about sex. We used a text called "The Facts of Life and Love." Each chapter began with a page devoted to a humorous cartoon with a caption. One cartoon showed a couple sitting on a park bench and embracing one another. The caption "Everything that's fun is either illegal, immoral or fattening."

In one of my presentations I told the group that one of the things I learned from keeping bees was the following: From time to time when a hive gets overcrowded the bees produce a new queen. The virgin queen takes off on her mating flight followed by a host of male bees. I explained how the first one to catch her mated the queen. He paid for his pleasure with his life. In the mating act he exploded and that was the end of him. Bill from Cape Breton stood up at the back of the room threw his arms in the air saying "boy what a way to go!"

Occasionally I read to those students, sections from the text book. One copy came with its cover on upside down. I would read from that copy. One of the young people would draw up sufficient courage to ask "How can you read so well while the book is upside down?" To which I would explain that I always read that way when I was dealing with my anxiety. At that point the students became more relaxed and open as we talked about sex.

In everyday life, whether in conversation with friends or pursuing some project together with another person, I delight in pointing out the comedy in a situation. I still enjoy recounting a funny story I have read or heard from another person. Here are three stories shared for your enjoyment.

Weddings are events where the comic can break forth unexpectedly. Rev. Earl McKnight the minister of a Baptist Church in Fredericton was leaving town to attend a course. He invited me to perform a wedding to which he had committed. There was no time for a rehearsal. As a substitute for the rehearsal, the wedding party and I met in the minister's study for instructions twenty minutes before the wedding was to begin.

The guests were all in the pews and the bride was waiting on the arm of her father in the vestibule. The groom, the best man and I entered from the choir end of the Church. As we took our positions and waited for the bridal party to come down the aisle, the groom started to put his foot and leg between my legs. In the office I had told him that he would be in the correct position while he waited for his bride to enter if he placed his left foot just in front of my left foot. Before the guests turned to watch the bride enter, their eyes saw the groom pushing his left leg well forward in between my legs .The groom was so nervous that he failed to understand why I pushed his leg away. He kept pushing. I was uncomfortable. What was the bride's father thinking as he witnessed this behaviour of his new son in law? Would he be concerned about the sexual orientation of the minister?

It was at a banquet of graduates from Pine Hill Divinity Hall when the speaker told a story that could have been about any of the guests when they arrive at their golden years. Reverend Stanley MacQueen's story was a prediction about the future state of many of his fellow ministers.

Two aged buddies did their weekly walk together in the neighborhood. They were both widowers and living on their own. One of them had been away for a month visiting with his daughter. On his return he got up early and set out on his familiar walk. He met his buddy along the way; "Your face is familiar. We have met here before but I don't remember your name, tell me what is your name?" To which his buddy, after thinking for a moment, replied "When do you need to know?"

And here is one of my favourite stories which contains both humour and wisdom. It was told at a regional meeting of pastoral counsellors. One of my peers recounted the story with respect for all present.

A mature social worker was commissioned by the agency where she worked to attend a conference on sexuality. Travel to the conference included a stopover with her Mom and Dad who still lived on the farm. She visited the home farm before and after the conference. When explaining to her parents that the conference would be about sex, there was considerable interest from both parents. Dad asked Charlotte "if you pick up any information that you think would be useful; when you come back on the weekend we would like to hear about it."

Charlotte returned four days later. When supper was over and they were sharing around the table there was considerable interest in what Charlotte learned at the conference. Dad was particularly interested and finally asked if she learned anything that would be of benefit to him. Charlotte's response was as follows: "Well Dad, there is bad news and there is good news. The bad news is that as you get older the times between sexual arousal get farther and farther apart." Dad was quick to ask "And what's the good news?" With a mischievous smile Charlotte replied "The good news is that it takes longer for you to come." This allegory serves to illustrate a relationship between parent and adult offspring that has within it a soul friend quality.

In the sharing of that story, our group of middle-aged professionals was facing the fact of change in our lives. The response from the group revealed an understanding of where we were heading.

Sharing humorous stories about the sexual side of life is no longer acceptable in our politically correct culture. Humour was helpful in the culture in which I grew up. Funny stories about sex and seeing the comic in certain situations provided an outlet for sexual expression during my growing up years. When I dated Mary, my parents knew that this resource helped me to wait until my wedding night.

Many of us waited until the night of our marriage for our first real sexual bonding by way of intercourse. And when it happened to me I had the thought that God himself was smiling with delight. Now I know for an inner certainty that God rejoices with me.

Spicing sermons with an excess of humour may be an indication of a lack of quality training in homiletics. Are we to measure success in ministry by the volume and number of laughs the minister produces in sixty minutes? It appears to me that one minister I know utilizes that technique for building her ego when depressed because of the dwindling numbers in the pews. To be fair, the practice is linked to the success of comedy television shows. Comedy television is for entertainment. Stand-up comics in the pulpit show poor judgment. I would rather be out communing with nature than be a captive audience of a minister who gets in the way of the soul bonding between me and God. These ministers leave no room for the Soul of the Universe to connect with the congregation.

As you have noticed my soul has just moved on from its humorous side to a cynical touch. There is a dualism between my cynicism and my humour. My soul helps me to find a balance between the two sides; humour and a positive outlook on life always win out.

Soul Adapts to Change

Nothing that is can pause or stay;
The moon will wax, the moon will wane,
The mist and cloud will turn to rain,
The rain to mist and cloud again,
Tomorrow be today.
            Henry Wadsworth Longfellow

Change is a constant in the journey we travel. Some changes happen gradually. The speed of change has increased incrementally over the span of my life. Reflecting on the past three decades of my journey, I found that any effort to measure either the sum total or speed of change in my world is beyond measurement. Nurturing one's soul is a necessity, and not an option, if one wishes to maintain a balanced life. The exercise of reflecting on my journey brought the changes into focus. This essay is a partial account of what I discovered. I hope that your reflection will be as good for your soul as it has been for mine.

What would it be like for my mother, who in 1925 has just placed the receiver back on the old party-line telephone. It is a 10x20x7 inch box that is screwed to wall of her kitchen. She is suddenly transported from 1925 to 2010. Imagine her thoughts when on the steps of the Musquodoboit Rural High School she witnesses a student talking into a smart phone? Challenging the cold March winds, many of these modern girls (would be showing portions of their bellies) dressed in keeping with the latest fad. Dressed in blouses and jeans they reveal three inches of their bellies. Their jeans reveal the cracks between the cheeks of their buttocks. My mother would find it difficult to understand that this fad is an important rite of passage for adolescents. Only a well established soul, accustomed to change, could escape being completely confused.

My mother's first reaction would be to think that she was in an entirely different country. Then, realizing that this is Musquodoboit, the experience would leave her in a temporary surrealistic mode. Would her rational and emotional system suddenly freeze up as does my laptop on occasion when the messages entering the system are beyond its capability?

Changes that take place over very short time frames cause us to sit up and take notice. We can be sidetracked away from our destination. Our souls play a function in keeping us on track. In moments of reflection, two incidents of surrealistic experiences emerge on my memory screen. One was on my return from London following a tour of Scotland and England after a conference in Edinburgh. The flight across the Atlantic to Halifax was uneventful. On deplaning at the airport and for about an hour afterwards I was in this surrealistic mode. Yet my system did not shut down. Reconnecting with family and friends restored my sense of reality. This experience was a soul event and not simply limited to body, mind and emotions. I have been on several

other major flights such as Bombay to London,
Vancouver to Narita airport in Japan. San Francisco to
New Zealand, Vancouver to Fiji. On none of these
transfers into new situations did I find myself in a
temporary freeze up.

One other incident resulted in a strong sense of
surrealistic feelings and thoughts. My soul was
impacted in a striking way. I was going from
Tatamagouche, Nova Scotia to Southwestern
Massachusetts. Prior to driving to the Halifax airport,
I was acting as a consultant to three leaders who were
about to conduct a laboratory in human relations at
the Atlantic Christian Training Centre. Back in the
1960's human relations labs were popular, both in the
United Church and to a degree in the corporate
world. The leaders of this particular lab were in a
state of confusion and were mucking around in their
own mini lab. Due to certain negative results of their
leadership they did not get their feet out of the bog
over the next ten days. Fortunately I was able to
extract myself after one day because I was committed
to flying to Boston and driving South from there. The
ice was still in the Northumberland Strait. Winter was
trying hard to hang on. In Boston I picked up my
rental car and as I drove South toward Connecticut I
suddenly realized that within a very brief time frame
I was surrounded by flowers and shrubs in full
bloom. This whole experience was a major change
from one surrealistic group experience, that of the
laboratory, to the practical tasks of getting to Boston. I
was thrust into another space. Certainly I was not

prepared for the change. I had mistakenly anticipated that the Tatamagouche weather would go with me.

The impact on my soul of most of the changes over the past eight and a half decades has been gradual, yet significant. The changes emerge into my consciousness at times when I long for "the good old days." Such longings tend to trick us into thinking that the good old days were always glorious and without stress. As I ease into the mood of reflecting and writing I find that my soul seems to immerse me back into those earlier experiences without the longing for the good old days. Sometimes it lasts for mere minutes, at others even for an hour or two. Going back usually brings enjoyment and satisfaction. It is like experiencing change in reverse. The then becomes the now. My soul has been so well nourished, together with a good set of genes, that I have not returned to the sad unhappy experiences of my life, of which there have been several. I know that I have much to be grateful for and have been more fortunate than several of my friends and members of my family.

Recalling and reflecting on the impact on my soul of some of the major changes over the decades has been positive. My soul has been nourished while writing about my journey. Also the family reunions of 2005 and 2010 served up rich food for the soul.

Back on the farm we did not seem to mind that we had no alternative to sitting on an ice cold toilet seat before setting out to the barn to do the morning chores. Fortunately our outhouse was attached to the wood house, saving us from having to walk through the snow. There was no disposal field system. One of my tasks as a teenager on a twice yearly basis was to empty the storage area beneath those seats. The contents were spread over the field for fertilizer. Today that silage from septic tanks is processed and spread on lawns in the city and on vegetable gardens from which the harvest shows up in the natural food section of the super store. Reflection warns me to avoid the natural food areas.

For years there was no indoor bathroom. Our Saturday night baths were in a large portable tub. In cold weather other family members vacated the kitchen while one of us took our bath. The water was heated in large pots on the kitchen stove. Even though we had a good furnace and plenty of wood, for comfort the kitchen was the best choice. When I went off to University living at Pine Hill was my choice of residence. That was a new and a welcome experience. No more feces to shovel. Warm porcelain seats that fitted your bottom better than the round hole cut in the wooden seat of the outhouse. We had real toilet paper in place of the pages of the newspaper or worse still the Simpsons catalogue.

At times, I stop to think about the scientific achievements over the next century. My thoughts are interrupted by recalling how the world's largest collection of books was burned in the ancient city of Alexandria. I am continually amazed by how we humans have found ways to destroy those few but memorable advances that were achieved long before the invention of the printing press. Only to be wiped out by war or religious conflicts. We have made unthinkable strides over the past thirty years, might we just as easily and in an equally short time frame, destroy our achievements?

God said "Let there be light," and there was the sun and the moon. I think about some of the changes between that event and the day when I arrived on the scene. The greatest progress prior to my birth came with the invention of the printing press. Could it be that the greatest progress between when I was born in 1922 and now will have been the invention of the digital age. Will this digital world implode upon us?

My Dad had installed a gasoline powered generator in the basement area beneath the porch of our house. We had electric lights while ninety-five percent of our neighbours used kerosene lamps and lanterns. When the generator broke down, we resorted to the kerosene lamp or used candles. We made candles from paraffin wax. The wax was from the same kerosene source. Then came the depression and there was not enough money either to repair the machinery nor to buy fuel for the generator. Thus we were forced to do our lessons by the light of a lamp. Carrying a lantern around the barn, while feeding hay to the cattle, required careful training about being cautious with fire. Barn fires in the valley were predominantly caused by combustion from storing poorly cured hay in the hay mow. I never heard of a barn fire in those days caused by a farmer through careless use of the lantern.

A severe thunder storm was a worry for rural people. Before lightning rods came to the valley a lightning strike could wipe out a house or barn in short time. When lightning rods were first invented by a Bostonian, most ministers and priests in Massachusetts came out in opposition to their use. Man must not interfere with God's plans. Did that opposition and reasoning prevent their use in Musquodoboit for a generation or two?

Dress for the boys was different in those early days, yet there is a familiar ring. Most boys attending the Greenwood school wore jeans. These were the poor man's pants. I do not recall that the girls ever wore jeans. They were expected to wear skirts or dresses. Today both men and women pay big dollars for jeans. Partly because the jeans feel like an extra layer of skin and you can maintain the contours of your body for onlookers. Today the sons of the men who wear eight hundred dollar suits wear jeans to university. In the winter we wore larrigans, leather footwear copied from the natives.

There was no competition with your peers. I recall how excited I was one Christmas getting my first pair of larrigans. They all looked the same, being totally devoid of style. These larrigans had to be kept oiled to prevent getting wet feet. About the twenty fourth of May, or when the frogs began peeping, both sexes were allowed to go to school in their bare feet. Recently the finance minster of British Columbia was criticized for wearing six hundred dollar shoes the day she presented her budget in the legislature.

The girls who bare their bellies and the lads who wear pants with the crotch starting at the height of their knees are currently in step with fashion. Both sexes are making sexual statements. A sexual message is being expressed by these girls. They are expressing a traditional, but unconscious motive of tantalizing the men. I would surmise that the men are stating that their penis is long and big, requiring extra space for storage. If in the future when they have to resort to Viagra, will they admit to their partners that they hadn't needed those baggy pants after all? Or will they secretly feed on Viagra and still wear them?

As a lad, I was never exposed to gala events such as the Academy Awards viewed by millions every year. I would assume, though, that the high fashion dress at the New Year's levees held at the lieutenant governor's mansion in Halifax would not hold a candle to the fashion display at the Academy Awards ceremony today. Family and friends would agree that I have never been much of a high dresser. Would I be able to fit in at one of the many parties that follow the Academy Award ceremony?

Shopping for groceries has undergone a significant change. There were three main sources from which we secured supplies that ended up on the dining room table or in our lunch pails that we carried off to the woods. The chief of these three sources of food was the farm itself. Most of our meat was raised on our farm except for rabbits snared in the winter. If those supplies dried up, then Campbell Brown distributed meat that was raised on other

farms in the valley. Our meat was kept cool buried
under sawdust on ice in the ice house, or it was salted
down to become corned beef. We caught a few fish
but mostly for pleasure. During certain seasons a
fisherman from the Eastern shore went through
peddling fresh fish. Mackerel were the usual fare.
Lobsters were unheard of. We always grew our own
vegetables in a well tended garden. We had sufficient
supplies of potatoes, parsnips, carrots, squash and
beets to carry over until the new crop came on in the
summer and early fall. These vegetables were stored
in the basement of the house. Apples were in fairly
good supply from our orchard.

　　We were not much as hunters but great at being
gatherers. Every summer the whole family was
engaged in picking wild strawberries, then
raspberries and finally blueberries. Enough jams,
jellies and preserves were processed to keep the
family in supply for the following year. During the
actual berry picking season a portion of our wild
berries was made into sumptuous pies. I was about
ten years old before strawberry plants were
introduced and the berries harvested. Even today I
enjoy picking wild cranberries and blueberries. I go to
farm fields to pick raspberries, strawberries and
blueberries. The surplus goes into my freezer in
Musquodoboit and West Vancouver. For me, the
gathering of berries has not been replaced by
shopping for them in the local super store. My soul is
still at work in maintaining a balance in my life.

The local source for the supplies that were not grown on the farm was P.G. Archibald's general store, a fifteen minute walk from home. My Dad ran an account there. When the bill got high and demands for payment were made, we would slaughter a cow or a pig and take the carcass to the store as payment. When I became a teenager I occasionally did the slaughtering. The year Dad was ill I did most of that necessary work. One occasion I recall was when I had to kill and process our big bull. Could I strike him hard enough in the correct spot to knock the animal unconscious on the first blow? Today the provincial department of health would require that we have a permit to process our own meat.

Our wholesale supplies of food came by way of the train. These staples would be ordered from a firm in Dartmouth. The train would unload the packages, bags and barrels into the little station down at the corner of our field. Helping to pick up these supplies, bringing them to the house and inspecting them was a time of excitement galore. Molasses came in a big barrel to which we attached a spigot. Cheese came packaged in a round box made of wood. The total weighed some forty pounds. Tea came in a cube shaped box about thirty inches square. The box was lined with lead to keep the tea fresh. As I recall, flour was in large hemp bags weighing one hundred pounds. Then there was corn meal, which the family used on the one hand for making porridge for breakfast, and on the other for feeding the pigs. We made a brew cooked in a big cauldron over an open fire in the yard, not the same tub in which we had our Saturday night bath; not to worry, the fire was safely in the kitchen stove on those nights. Oatmeal porridge was standard fare for breakfast. Today I get my supply of oatmeal from the bins of the supermarket store to make granola; my grandson Alec claims that my granola is the very best. This is likely the closest this young lad from the new millennium generation will ever get to eating cornmeal mash brewed for pigs. By the way I prefer the home made granola. Like some of my friends, it is my choice of cereal most mornings.

The railway from Dartmouth to Musquodoboit is now gone. O'Brien's wholesale firm in Dartmouth has been replaced by a supermarket. You, the reader, can fill in just how much things have changed by reflecting on your own current pattern of shopping for staples. Back in the days of my youth there was no shopping for discretionary goods. There was no extra money allowing us to make such choices. How much has the pattern of your shopping for discretionary goods changed over time? Have you been brainwashed by the media and flyers deposited in your mailbox? Do you resort to reckless buying? If you have protected yourself from the influence of advertising and still have had fun choosing to buy some luxury item, then it will have been good for your soul.

Imagine the excitement when my grandmother invited me and my sister to come around to her suite in our farmhouse. We took turns putting on the

headphones of her new radio, and listening to the Ho
Ho Ho's of Santa Claus. I assume that her radio, run
by a battery, was little more than a crystal set. This
morning I sat by the fireplace in our living room
reading from my kindle e-reader. With the touch of
the screen I connected wirelessly with the kindle store
miles away in Washington State.

This afternoon, while I write, I'm also listening to
Beethoven's Ode To Joy. I have imported the ninth
symphony from a CD into the iTunes program on my
computer. When I go to the woods to shear my
Christmas trees I can listen to the same music from
my iPod, stored in my shirt pocket.

Because of amazing advances in digital and
wireless communication we are informed within
minutes of a tragedy occurring on the opposite side of
our planet. Seventy years ago while my Mom and
Dad were away on a brief holiday in their car, three
men were trapped in the Moose River gold mine,
which was fourteen miles from the farm. Within a day
after the mine caved in, a Halifax radio station set up
equipment for broadcasting from the site. That was
the very first on-site reporting effort to inform the
world about any such event. Frank Willis caught the
interest and imagination of people in many countries
around the world. This was the real stuff. A man's
voice, loaded with expression and feelings, influenced
not only the interest but the emotions of millions of
individuals, many of whom hardly knew where to
find Canada on the globe, let alone the small village
of some forty people that is called Moose River .

Watching workers and machines attempting to locate and find people buried in their homes by an earthquake far away in Haiti is an experience within another dimension. A strong soul is helpful in making the distinction between news and entertainment. Even tragedies are sometimes presented as entertainment. Unless the reporters send the news out as entertainment, their TV stations may drop in the ratings and lose advertisers. Not only have the airwaves acquired a global dimension, so has the bottom line of many financial statements. It is my contention that every high school could contribute to making the world a more honest place. A few courses could be taught in how to sort out the news from the entertainment. What better teaching tool than the TV at news time. Stop the action and examine the content from a critical perspective.

On reflection I return to that evening when I watched my first movie, a Charlie Chaplin comedy. The brief script was written at the bottom of the screen. There was no sound. Within the next month I will watch a movie in an IMAX theater. The wrap around screen and sound that encompasses my soul will enable me to sense that I am part of the event I'm watching. My soul seems to be able to adapt and I return to the real world as I walk out through the doors of the theater.

A skilled psychiatrist may at times advise his patient that it is OK to remain in the world of hallucinations. I remember riding with Bennett Wong, a well know Vancouver psychiatrist. This happened on my way to catch a ferry to present at a conference on Vancouver Island. I was riding with Dr. Wong. His patient called him about a hallucination she was having at the moment. I assume that because she was suicidal he had given her his cellular telephone number. His advice was, "there is nothing to fear. Enjoy those thoughts when they come. Not everybody has the opportunity. Try doing a few kitchen chores and you will return to the reality around you."

I wonder about how the soul adapts to change. It is one of life's mysteries. I am forming the belief that our soul takes shape sometime between our conception and our exit from the womb. I think that from then on the soul is timeless into the future. Acquiring information appears to be at its peak during the stage of development that begins in the third year of life. Access to information has increased so rapidly over the decades that the soul may easily experience overload. Or we might conclude that it is the soul that protects us from freezing up from overload. In the same way that my laptop refuses to work at times.

Moving through those eleven grades in Greenwood school we had no library. When I first went to Dalhousie I had to learn how to use a library. Today students can go on the internet and obtain information to do their homework. Even with all my years of studies and gathering knowledge I frequently find myself turning to my grandchildren for answers to my 'how to' questions. Jonathan shows me how to build playlists on my iPod.

I think of that wonderful child's prayer, "If I should die before I wake, I pray the Lord my soul do take." What happens to all that acquired knowledge when I die? I have spent a lifetime putting it all together in order to make sense of it. I wonder if there is more than simply passing it on to future generations in a book, as I am doing as I write.

All of the changes recorded here have emerged into consciousness by reflecting on my life experiences. What part has my soul played in influencing my adaptation to those changes? I sense that my soul assists me in remaining flexible and maintaining openness as I grow older. The exercise of reflecting on the changes over my lifetime brought to the fore changes that are dramatic.

I could produce a whole book on the changes over the past eight decades and I would still wonder about the place of my soul in adapting to them. You, the reader, can write your own paragraphs, the same as you would when watching a movie without the benefit of sound.

The table of contents of my book would include interesting comparisons.

Christmas concerts in the one room school in the
    1930's
The production of Annie in the rural high school in 2005

The thrill of seeing a small prop plane fly over our
    farm in 1934
Watching a supersonic plane fly over Vancouver in 1986

Blackboards and chalk for writing
Word processors and laptops

Logging, using cross cut saws, axes and horses
Tree processors and log porters

Five people needed to run a farm
Arthur Kent manages his larger farm alone in 2005

Baling Christmas trees by hand
Baling with a power driven Howie baler in 2004

A Charlie Chaplin movie, with no sound and subtitles
Watching a movie in an Imax theatre

Skiing with work boots secured by bear claw bindings
Ski boots that adjust to the contours of your foot

Crokinole, checkers and card games for home
    entertainment
TV on a large high definition screen and computer games

Hearing or reading stories from the Holy Scriptures
Taking your son to soccer and hockey games on Sunday

Securing heat for the home uses 20% of a farmer's
    labour
It takes a few minutes each month to pay the heating bills

Burying pond ice in sawdust for summer
    refrigeration
Reminding your kids to close the fridge door

If I were to write a book on change, the final
chapter would focus on the impossibility of
measuring both the speed and amount of change over
the past three decades. Changes in the next three
decades might happen faster than a digital search
program can find the word 'change' in these essays.
Some of those changes can throw our lives into
imbalance. There is much to be grateful for when I
focus on the positive impact of these changes on our
daily lives. However it is frightening when I focus on
the negative consequences. The speed of those
changes can throw our lives into imbalance. Burnout,
stress and dissatisfaction with what we have already
and striving for more while we have enough create an
imbalance. There is no time or energy left to reflect on
the core values of our lives. A balanced life includes
time to connect with both the soul of nature and the
Soul of the Universe. It is our soul that provides the
energy necessary for maintaining a healthy balance.
    Tradition pulls at my coattails, urging me to get
grounded and balanced. In today's world we are
challenged by endless advertising, using seductive
words to choose the advertiser's products. Then my

soul challenges me to take the healthy route when making choices. When I am tempted to give in to their seduction, my soul encourages me to return to the core values of my life. My soul reminds me that I can make better choices. There were a few times when I made the wrong choice. My soul assisted me in getting back on the right track.

Through this exercise of reflecting on my journey I have come to an open door toward understanding how the soul manages change. My soul, the soul of nature and the soul of the universe (God) work together to assist me in moving out of the imbalance caused by rapid change. I am able to move to the core values of my soul, thus avoiding overload and imbalance. In some mysterious way my soul is interconnected with those other two souls. Functioning together they have protected me from the damage caused by rapid change.

Together they have opened doors for me that enable me to take advantage of particular changes. There are those times when I gave in to curiosity and the results have enriched my soul. The curious side of my soul confronted me with 'what's on the other side of the mountain?' Let's hike up further and take a look. The consequences of my choices can be seen throughout these essays. My soul helped me in maintaining a balance, even when I found myself on a slippery moss covered slope.

Imprinted on the recesses of my mind is a picture of my eldest grandson who placed himself where he could protect me from getting hurt. We were high up

on Whistler Mountain. We were crossing a steep and
rocky slope. The centre of gravity tugged at us in a
way that would plunge us into the ravine below. As I
clung to one rock, and then another, to keep from
falling I stopped to size up the situation. I noticed that
Micah had chosen to move from rock to rock
immediately below me. Neither of us spoke of his
move. Yet we both knew that his move was
intentional. In a like manner the soul does not
broadcast its moves. It is there silently reminding us
of the relationship between our souls, the soul of
nature and the soul of the universe (God).

PART II

CAREER CHOICES
IMPACTED BY SOUL

Essay 10

When Making Career Decisions

How many colours are in your rainbow? In the early part of the twenty first century one's career choices are not limited to the colours of the rainbow. Instead of choosing from one or two colour charts on which to walk up and over the rainbow, the situation is more like looking down on a chart of colours in a Colours Your World store on main street. Today you are confronted with a plethora of choices.

The paths available to me were limited to fewer than the colours of the rainbow. On reflection, it seems that unlike today, there were few forks in the road where along the way I could veer in another direction. The choices that you make in the future in deciding which fork in the road you take will depend on how well you are caring for your soul. The notes that you make from researching your choices will not be enough. It will take more. Utilizing your soul will embrace all of you, mind, emotions, spirit and your body.

There were no millennium scholarships. Nor was there a local non-governmental organization providing financial support. Governments and the Coca Cola's of the day wanted cheap labour. They wanted men, women and children who would be the hewers of wood and drawers of water. There was no encouragement for me to go to university. What direction could a young person follow?

There was no financial encouragement. After I made my decision about going to Dalhousie University my Dad sold off one of his beef cattle to assist with my expenses. Only infrequently was I able to fall back on small gifts of cash from Dad. He did not have the money, in spite of the many hundreds of acres of woodland he owned. My source of income for college days was to work in the summers and borrow money from Stuart Archibald. During post graduate days Lillian was the chief breadwinner.

There were models to follow when I finished grade eleven. I might have been inspired by the example of Florence Rhind or Dorothy Taylor, two of my teachers. I would have chosen teaching as my career; possibly without any formal training. On reflection I believe that Dorothy Taylor may have inspired her female students to follow the normal career choice in those days. Dorothy left teaching, found a husband, got married and raised children.

As the oldest son I would have chosen farming in keeping with family tradition. Another avenue that appealed to me was to follow in the footsteps of my father's brother, my uncle Tim. Uncle Tim had taken a business course in Halifax and worked for Canada Customs. My skill with numbers and my imagination about the soul of the Royal Bank which had a local branch in Middle Musquodoboit were the forces pulling me in that direction.

I had completed my education in the little one room school. My Dad was not well and was ordered to bed for a heart condition. I found myself pretty well resigned to staying on the farm. My brother Seymour was almost three years younger. Expectations that Seymour would manage the farm were not under consideration. My opinion of him as a worker was embedded in the phrase "Seymour (see more) and do less." Little did I know that he turned out to be as much of a workaholic as his older brother John.

I reflect on my career choices. How different my life would have been if I had decided to go the route of the financial world, or followed in the footsteps of my father as a farmer. I would not now be basing my stories on a soul theme. By chance I may have read Thomas Moore's books. My first introduction to his writings was by a cherished soul friend who was a social worker. I understand now that living and working on a farm close to nature provided a fine opportunity for soul making. Would that choice have permitted me to acquire a maturing understanding of Soul?

If I had not pulled away from the forces pulling me to remain on the farm, how different my life may have been. Looking at what might have been, from the perspective of health alone. My brother Seymour had open heart surgery recently. Long lasting heart and lung problems have plagued his ageing process. Nature has its dark side. Seymour has suffered from the results of hard work, farm dust and smoking.

Genetically our family may have been vulnerable. I recall reports from my mother that two of my grandfather Reid's sisters had tuberculosis. My

youngest brother Leslie was hospitalized for a time as
a young man with tuberculosis. The story of my
exposure to cigarette smoke is very simple. I tried
smoking one cigarette during that period between
school and University. I did not like the taste. I tried
one more while I was in college and my tastes did not
change. My choice not to smoke was not a moral or
health issue. For a period, while working in the
canteen at Pine Hill Divinity Hall I was close to being
addicted to a combination of chocolate bars and milk.

    The health arena is only one aspect of my life that
benefitted from my choices. In other ways my soul
might have been different in degrees nearing 180 on
the compass. Consider the political spectrum as one
other area. I'm not clear on how much of a red Tory
my father was. I do recall that on one occasion he
broke from the tradition of his family, which always
voted Conservative. I had been on a mission field for
the United Church in Saskatchewan, the birthplace of
the social party of Canada. I was influenced by J. S.
Wordsworth and Tommy Douglas. Following my
return from Saskatchewan I decided to campaign in a
Federal election. I persuaded my Dad to host a lawn
party for the CCF. I wonder now if my Dad came
close to having a heart attack as he folded his ballot to
put it in the box. The pressure from the numerous
other Stewarts in the valley for him to vote in keeping
with the party line would have been enormous. I
wonder if he voted for the Tory candidate after all. I
doubt it. It would have been just as difficult for his

relatives to undergo such a change of heart as it was for his son to persuade him to host that lawn party.

Supposing I had gone to business school in Halifax and was able to get a position with the Royal Bank. How different my life would have turned out to be. How far up the corporate ladder would I have climbed? How many rungs of my soul would have broken under the stress and weight of the responsibilities? As a male I may have had more opportunities to climb that ladder than Beverly Redden, who retired from the Royal Bank in the summer of 2004. After working there for years, Beverly retired from working in the small Musquodoboit branch. Her husband Harley retired at the same time from his work. Harley was key to the success of Conform Limited, a newly formed silviculture co-operative. These two people deserve rewards for their contributions to the community.

Just now it is time to face you as reader with two questions. What one or more events stand out for you as a clear turning point in the career path which you are traveling? In what way was your soul involved?

My soul was involved in one major event that was a turning point in my life. The time it took for the event to happen was just as fleeting. Yet the event is as clear as though it happened yesterday. The one event that was a turning point was as follows. It was in the Summer of nineteen thirty-nine before the outbreak of World War II. It was haying time on the farm. I had driven three miles to my grandfather Reid's to pick up some article for use in the farm work. Time was of the essence. I was walking from the back door of my Grandfather's house to return to my car. On that short walk, our minister John Ball was on his way in for a pastoral visit. He stopped me for a moment and asked if I had ever thought of going into the ministry. I remember that my answer was no and brushed him aside with the fact that I was in a hurry. I thought that I had completely forgotten his query. But the seed was sown. Later, John Ball's soul connected with mine and we became soul friends. A year later over the Winter and the following Spring I home studied Physics and Greek as a second language. John Ball became my tutor on weekly visits to his home. I wrote provincial exams in Middle Musquodoboit in both subjects and passed with flying colours thanks to my tutor. In mid July I, along with other grade eleven students from several schools in the valley, waited impatiently for the results to arrive in the mail. On the day my envelope arrived I read the results with very mixed feelings. I had a grade of 98 for Physics with no report for the Greek exam. A day or two later I had a call from Dorothy Blaikie, the daughter of the manager of the creamery in Middle Musquodoboit. She was mistakenly credited with the marks for my Greek exam. Dorothy told me on the phone that I had achieved a 90 on that exam. With an excellent teacher like my minister and plenty of motivation, home schooling worked well for me.

A short time later Dorothy and I began dating. She was working as a telephone operator in the old fashioned telephone office in Middle Musquodoboit. When I returned to Dalhousie, the telephone was our main method for arranging dates. There was no smart phone for texting. We never really became soul friends. I do recall with satisfaction that the long distance charges were always waived.

As I reflect on the process of my career choice, my soul was at work. Having faced various career choices early on, I was well prepared for changes along the journey. There is more elsewhere about my change from regular parish ministry to establish a Lay Training Centre in Tatamagouche. Another change took me to Boston University to prepare myself as a pastoral counsellor. On graduation from that program I moved across the continent to establish a pastoral counselling centre. On retirement I built up a Christmas tree business.

My soul was nourished in many ways during each of those careers. The experiences in one setting opened the doors for the next. For example, the counselling needs of some of the people who became involved in the programs at the Atlantic Christian Training Centre were beyond my skills and training. Acknowledgment of this shortcoming was a major factor in my decision to return to post graduate studies.

Reflecting on the process of making my career choices, I am surprised at the role of my soul throughout. I chose not to travel the road to farming. Over the past twenty years I have been farming Christmas trees. One of the career options was the road that led to a career in the business world. I decided against following in the footsteps of my uncle. There was no business school on the road I would take. In my retirement, I now hold shares in three Canadian banks. There are other securities in our portfolios which I manage personally. My soul has played a role in assisting me in fulfilling dreams that might have been.

In the ebb and flow between my soul and my career choices, was my soul active in building a career that has been fulfilling for me as a person? Did my soul know which road I would take while I was still a mile away from the junction where I would make a decision? The essays on finances, farming and Christmas trees provide some answers. The soul was the link between the then of farming and the now of trees and money. In between there were many years of studies and a ministry of caring about and for souls.

Weather and Soul Interact

*When human beings lose their connection to
nature, to heaven and earth, then they do not know
how to nurture their environment or how to rule
their world -which is saying the same thing.*
Chogyam Trungpa

How many times in a week does the weather make a
difference to your plans? During the years on the
farm in Musquodoboit I learned to read the weather
and to respect weather conditions. My soul became
attuned to nature through these acquired skills.

It was much easier to predict the weather while
working on the farm seventy years ago, than it is
now. Weather patterns were more consistent. Even
the Farmer's Almanac could depend on a fairly stable
pattern. As farmers, we could begin haying in early
July. We could harvest the vegetables that had to be
stored before the first frost around the third week of
September. The wood had to be stored and the house
banked before the first heavy freeze up in November.
There would be snow for Christmas. We hoped for a
mild New Year's Day because it was customary to
butcher one of our beef cattle to provide meat for the
rest of the winter. One quarter or a side of that beef
went to Archibald's store as a payment on the
growing grocery and feed bill. We could expect a
January thaw. Winter would return the next week

with a vengeance. We could depend on transporting wood by team and sled over the frozen Musquodoboit River. The river separated the farm house from the woodlot where we cut our supply of hardwood for the next year. If there was water on top of the ice from the thaw, I had to encourage the horses to walk into the water. Before we reached home, their hooves and the runners of the bob sled were covered with ice.

There is a one-time event which is related to a January thaw. I recall that event with feelings of fear. Reflection informs me that I was protected by an unseen force. I had parked at my grandfather Reid's farm. The roads were glib with ice. When I returned to the car it would not start, not uncommon in those days especially during a thaw. George Fulton came along with the gas truck. George was the worker who had married my favourite and well loved teacher Dorothy Taylor. I accepted his offer to tow me the three miles back to the farm. We both discussed that the tow chain was mighty short for the task at hand. We decided to take the risk. On reflection I assume that he decided to give me a thrill, as dangerous as it would be. Or perhaps he had an unconscious need to get even with me for the soul mate relationship I had with my teacher Dorothy. George and Dorothy were courting at the time. Imagine the helpless feeling of this seventeen year old, sitting in that car swinging from side to side over the road behind a big truck that was loaded with gasoline. My survival was out of my control. Only a robot would not be afraid.

Many of the tasks on the farm were linked to the seasons. Nature's soul and my soul as a farmer established a spirit of cooperation. There was one group of daily tasks which had to be done regardless, rain or shine; milking the cows, separating the cream from the milk and feeding milk to the calves. There were occasions when I had done these chores on my own. I milked the cows by hand. A few days after the birth of a new calf we would wean it from its mother. A stubborn calf needed considerable persuasion when teaching it how to drink rather than suck. I had learned from my dad that you put two or three fingers into the mouth of the calf and then pushed its head under the milk in the pail. Sharp teeth tended to increase my frustration; at times the contest got into a win or lose situation. Could it be that the calf knew instinctively that I would not drown it in its mother's milk? Hunger pains were on my side. A small taste of milk, and the stubborn animal conceded and moved on toward maturity.

From the first of June through until mid-September, the cows were put out to pasture. Surrounding the clear cut areas where we had planted grass seed among the stumps, there were fifty acres of woods. The cows could find shelter from the heat and flies in the woods. Going to fetch the cows for the evening milking was another chore. Seldom did the cows come home of their own will. Swiss type cow bells were the norm for locating the cows. There were no digital ankle bracelets of the type that Martha Stewart is currently wearing following her discharge from prison. Occasionally, a cow would hide her new born calf in the woods. We knew something was up when an expectant cow was not with the herd. If she came home a few days later without her calf, then we had to set up a spy network to outsmart her in her genetic born tendency toward concealment. The soul of nature was providing an opportunity for my soul to grow my detective skills. Many years later, working with Christmas trees in those same woods provides a ready opportunity for the intertwining of the soul of nature with my soul.

There were two seasonal tasks which I did not like. Both were boring and the hours were long. Mother Nature's persistence, through actions of the winter frosts, was amazingly stone productive. Every Spring we had to pick a new crop of rocks. In the fields of Musquodoboit, unlike those of the Prairie Provinces or in the Peace River area of British Columbia, rocks grew in abundance. In those days the rocks were picked manually; today Arthur Kent has a machine which does it for him as he drives his air-conditioned tractor. Our task was back-breaking and it seemed so futile, because we knew that there would be another crop of rocks the following year. If you are curious about why the rocks return, I suggest that you do a bit of scientific research on Google; frost and moisture are the culprits.

The other task which was more boring, but felt less futile was weeding the turnip field. We grew three tons of turnips to feed the cattle. The turnips were sweet and they kept well in the turnip bin, which was a concrete extension of the cellar of the barn. Out in the field, rows were made with a holler, and the seeds planted with a mechanical gadget drawn by a horse. Seeds were cheap, and to ensure that no spaces were missed, several plants germinated on every foot of the row. It was my task to skillfully use a nine inch hoe to remove the extra plants without disturbing the roots of the selected plants. Although I detested this work, I still relish eating mashed sweet turnip served with chicken, fish or steak at supper.

There was one annual task that I enjoyed. Plowing the fields for next year's crop. We used a single furrow plow, drawn by a team of horses. Starting the first furrow in a large field taught me a lesson that has remained with me throughout the rest of my journey. I was trained to set the plow and then pick a point at the far end of the field, "Stay focused and keep your eye on your goal." It was easy to follow that instruction as I walked behind the plow; hands firmly on the handles, and looking ahead between the team of horses. It was only when I got to the end of the field that I adhered to the advice I received later from Chicken George "Son if you are going to know where you are going you have to know where you have been." Over a long day I could plow an acre.

Gathering the fuel used for cooking and heating was a big project on an annual basis. Today, people are complaining about how much the high cost of fuel is eating into their income. In the days when I was a farmer, it was not paying the fuel bill every month that was a problem. It was the amount of productivity time that was required for cutting, preparing and storing our wood. If a researcher were to do a project on the differences between then and now, the results would be startling. My guess would be that one fifth of every year was required out of a farmer's working year to provide fuel for the home, including the time it took to stoke the furnace and the kitchen stove.

The first step in this annual exercise was going to the woods to cut and pile the birch and maple trees. The Swede saw had not been invented so we went armed with a cross cut saw, axe and wedges. Each day we carried along our lunch. I remember sitting by an open fire on a cold winter day. My favourite delicacy was a sandwich made with fresh homemade bread. The filling would be pan-fried pork, homemade butter on the bread, with a dollop of molasses spread over the pork. The favourite sweet was doughnuts which we helped my mother make. I have yet to find any store bought doughnuts of equal quality.

At lunch time in the woods we regularly boiled the kettle over an open fire. If the snow was deep one made a hole in the snow for the fire. Water came either from a brook or spring, which sometimes required cutting a hole through the ice. Our boiling kettle was an oversized tin can with a handle made from hay wire. We used a freshly cut sapling to hold the kettle over the fire. When the water came to a boil, we would remove the pail from the fire and drop in the loose tea leaves. We did not know about tea bags. After adding the loose tea leaves, we would hold the pail over the fire again and bring it to the boil. This operation settled the leaves to the bottom of the pail. I was careful to remove the pail as soon as the bubbles appeared again, taking care not to boil it further. I have stopped drinking tea made by Fern, my brother Seymour's wife. Fern brought to their marriage a custom from her childhood in Debert, Nova Scotia. She boils her tea. Intensive boiling ruins tea. The result gives me an allergic reaction to the extra tannin leached out of the tea leaves.

The next step in processing our fuel was hauling it the mile long drive from the woods, to be piled in our back yard. Ordinarily, I drove a team of two horses hauling a set of bob sleds. One year I used a one horse sled to transport the wood. I recall that the yearly supply averaged twenty cords. Landed in the farm yard, the wood remained in neat piles until the next stage of processing. The wood had to be cut into two different lengths, one for the kitchen stove and the other for the furnace. By the time I began farming on a full time basis, the old cross cut saw was no longer in use. The age of machinery had advanced to the Swede saw. Productivity increased dramatically with one worker on each end of the saw. It required a fair amount of skill to get the rhythm of the back and forth movement of the saw. One had to learn how to avoid putting pressure on the teeth of the saw. With a sharp saw its own weight was more than what was required.

Along the way I had picked up the skill for sharpening all kinds of tools: axes, both cross cut and Swede saws, hand saws, cutter bars, etc. We cut the wood up with a circular saw. It was powered by a two-stroke gasoline engine. This operation required three people, two to load the wood onto the bench and to push the wood into the saw and a third person threw the separated piece of wood into a pile. This motor driven machine had moved mankind forward into another stage of the machine age. Back then, the chain saw was no more than a dream in the mind of some inventor.

The next step was to split the wood into sizes that would fit the furnace or the kitchen stove. The hardwood from the south side of the river was easier to split than its counterpart on the North side. Most blocks could be split asunder with an axe and without the aid of wedges. Hardwood from the hills North of the river was far harder to crack. The exercise of splitting the wood was not only to make the pieces fit the stove; opening up the wood was thought to increase the rapidity of curing the wood. I have learned since that most of the moisture in a stick of wood seeps out from the ends of the wood and not from the split faces of the stick. This makes sense because of the porous makeup of a tree. Sap moves up and down the length of the tree.

I enjoyed splitting wood. I recall with a smile a myth passed on years later by a much older neighbour in West Vancouver. Fred and his wife were intrigued by my splitting wood in the drive way of our home. They came across the street to observe and comment on my skills. My splitting skills had not diminished over the decades. With a chuckle and in a serious tone Fred remarked "A man's pecker is not fully grown until he can strike a stick of wood in the same place twice." Fred had never lived on a farm. By what process did this myth migrate to the city?

The wood for the kitchen stove was stored in the wood shed that was attached to the house. The furnace wood was stored in the basement of the house. We moved the wood to the house with a two-axle wagon and a team of horses. On one occasion I attached the family car to a two-axle wagon. Backing this contraption into a predetermined position was beyond the skills of my younger days.

Using the family car to tow a wagon full of wood was not a new experience. I learned to drive a car in the hay field. I was twelve years old. I drove while another worker sat on the rake and dumped the hay at the windrow. By the time I was fourteen I was driving the car on the highways. No license was required, and the rationale was that it was ethically permissible because I was driving to Church. After all I was teaching Sunday School, and with that sort of responsibility went the privilege of driving a car.

Harvesting the hay was a task that spanned five or six weeks. There have been major changes in the process. Arthur Kent has the kind of machinery that enables him to harvest and store triple the amount of hay in the same time span as we did years earlier. He does this alone. Using modern equipment, one man hour of work produces the same results as three man hours of work during my days in the hayfield.

I still like the smell of new mown hay. Decades later I can pick up the sweet scent of the August apples that we stored in the hay in the barn. The unripe apples were stored there for a few days so that the heat from the curing of the hay would hasten the ripening process. My reflection takes me back to times when my Dad played with me in the hay. The smell of new mown hay intermingles nicely with my memories of a Dad who played with me. Another gift from my soul!

My one negative experience with haying was getting a small hernia while moving hay from the hay loader up onto the wagon. I had to keep the back of the load free and open. The hay was heavy and with the steady movement of the wagon, this was a difficult task. The hernia was small enough to heal on its own. I was not so fortunate at seventy-five years of age when lifting a heavy baled Christmas tree. I made the mistake of not placing myself in the proper position to hoist the tree to my shoulder. This time surgery was necessary to repair the damage.

Dinner breaks at noon were welcome after working in the field. Unless there was a threat of rain these breaks lasted for an hour. I assume the horses appreciated their breaks. As workers we found ourselves on the verandah of the farm house. The old hammock was the first choice for a place to rest. On a very hot day we would take a short break in mid afternoon. The stop was brief, but long enough to enjoy a hot drink. The favourite drink, which was believed to cool one's body, was a hot one. The mixture was oatmeal and molasses in hot water. Today, we are pressured by clever advertising to purchase cold drinks filled with sugar. I have often noticed how the big stores are persuaded to put the Cocoa Cola coolers alongside the packages of salted potato chips; on checking I found that some varieties of chips are made and packaged by Cocoa Cola. Good marketing, but not as nutritious as our oatmeal drink on the farm.

Following two weeks of sunshine and perfect hay weather, a rainy day was most welcome. It seemed like it was a gift we deserved and had earned. We did not make hay on Sunday.

I reflect on a Sunday in early June. I was allowed to have the car to go to visit my soul friend Mary. We set out for the Annapolis Valley, driving over the Rawdon Hills to see the apple blossoms. It was the weekend of the blossom festival. There's more in another section about the relationship that she and I had. It is sufficient to document here that our relationship during those three years added to my enjoyment of life on the farm. That enjoyment along with the satisfaction of having the responsibility of the farm created a fine venue for soul development. My decision to head off to college, after three years of farm life, was not an effort to get away from the farm. The magnetic force which pulled me away seemed to have come from the Soul of the Universe.

While weather patterns have changed through global warming, the farmers have had to adapt to those changes with new methods of farming. All efforts to control the weather through such experiments as seeding the clouds in times of drought have failed. Successful farmers in modern times watch the weather report diligently, either on the radio, TV, or the internet. No longer do they depend entirely on the older methods of watching for signs of change in the weather. Those older signs are summed up in sayings like "fog on the hill, water for the mill" or "rainbow at night the sailor's delight, rainbow in the morning sailors take warning." My brother Seymour utilizes a mix of the old and the new, yet he pretends that he only uses the old signs. He has added a number of sharp observations that he has gathered over the years. He likes to outsmart the professional weatherman. With assistance from media that is dedicated to entertainment rather than accuracy, weather reports are occasionally in error. At times Seymour is more accurate. When Seymour errs he simply moves on, continuing to use his mix which works well for him.

Most scientists know that controlling the amount of pollutants we disperse into the atmosphere is essential to arriving at a better balance in the weather conditions around the globe. The successful farmers have adapted to the weather. They purchase expensive machinery to do their farming. They watch the forecasts and do the work in hours rather than days. I know of one or two situations where

machinery is of no help. One of these is in the
harvesting of strawberries. If workers are in short
supply, and the weather turns wet, many berries rot
in the field. The reader will understand why the
weather is a familiar topic of conversation among
farmers.

Weather is a topic which often surfaces in
telephone conversations with my daughter Janelle.
Janelle and her family live and travel alongside one of
British Columbia's longest and most dangerous
rivers. The Skeena river enters Hecate Strait on the
Southern outskirts of the city of Prince Rupert. Janelle
drives on the Yellowhead highway which ekes out
just enough land mass along the river to allow cars
and trucks to meet. Little wonder that the weather is a
serious topic in those conversations. Never does a
Winter end without road conditions having claimed
the life of a neighbour, the parents of a student they
teach or another teacher. Janelle and Neal have been
in the North for some twenty eight years. They know
the area much better than the bureaucrats who made
the decision to privatize the maintenance of the
highways. The bottom line for the companies that
have the responsibility for maintaining the roads
becomes more important than the safety and lives of
the drivers using them.

During the three years between graduating from
the one room school-house, and packing my bags to
leave home to attend Dalhousie University, even the
weatherman never heard about global warming.
Today in Nova Scotia as in British Columbia there are

sudden deviations from the weather patterns of the nineteen-thirties. Hurricane Juan in Nova Scotia in 2003 was one of them. That same year a deluge of rain in April washed out a bridge over School House brook in Elmsvale. The provincial transportation department farmed out the rebuilding of the bridge. The brook was hardly big enough to provide a home for the small ten-inch brook trout I fished from it when I was a boy. The contractor from away who built the new bridge. went bankrupt after spending fourteen million dollars. Poor planning and unpredictable weather combined to increase the costs twofold over estimates.

It is now a certainty that our current problem with global warming is caused by man-made emissions. Any final arguments put forth by oil and coal barons are now like the soap bubbles floating from a child's pipe only to burst in the wind. Greed has been the root cause of decades of delay in arriving at this certain conclusion. Do we have enough ingenuity, together with compassion for the soul of nature to avoid unimaginable disaster for our great grandchildren?

When the greed and ingenuity of men lead them to tamper with rather than cooperate with the soul of nature, tragedy often results. The famous Moose River mine disaster provides a wonderful illustration of how tampering with nature can be disastrous. The same tragedy illustrates how human ingenuity and sacrifice, working closely with the soul of nature brings success and rejoicing. The Moose River mine was only eleven miles from my home.

It was Easter Sunday in April 1936 when two greedy men, accompanied by their timekeeper, descended into the McGill shaft to explore and extract precious samples of gold from the supporting rock that held up the roof of the tunnel. I was but a farm lad approaching the age of fourteen. This tragedy had a big impact on my soul. Recollection informs me that my Mom and Dad were away the first two or three of those twelve eventful days. Dr. Robertson and Scadding were rescued. The third man, Mr. McGill, died of pneumonia on the seventh day of his underground entombment.

I had extra farm chores to do, yet there was time to listen to the radio. My interest in the hourly radio reports of the rescue operation was intensified because of my Dad's recent involvement in digging a mine shaft a short distance from the cave-in. I remember seeing fairly large nuggets of gold brought to our home. I recall seeing one brick of the final product that would have been the size of an old bar of surprise soap. In today's' market those fifty or sixty ounces of gold would more than pay off the farmer's loan that Dad took out to mine that gold. Both my brother Seymour and I remember crawling up the narrow shaft, step by step with Dad closely behind. The rock ore was hoisted up in a big bucket sliding up that same ladder. Attached to the bucket was a wire cable at the end of which was a horse, hundreds of feet above providing the horsepower.

The hourly reports of the rescue, made on site by
Frank Willis were broadcast from a Halifax radio
station. This was the very first ever in the history of
broadcasting of on-scene reporting. One newspaper
based in Stellarton, Nova Scotia, midway through the
rescue operation, falsely began a rumor that there was
a second cave-in and hundreds of volunteers died.
This rumor was made up by greedy, profit orientated
owners of the newspaper. Accuracy did not matter.
CNN and Fox are experts at this game. In 1936 the
small town paper intended to capitalize on the
fascination of millions of people in North America
and Europe. Frank Willis in Moose River had signed
off for the night. He reopened his broadcast
immediately and repeatedly denied the rumor (by
which time a few hundred stations in the United
Stated had picked up and run with the story). Last
night, many years later I listened to a tape of that
particular denial.

The lines from Rudyard Kipling's poem *The Sons
of Martha* has been quoted to describe another aspect
of the tragedy: "Simple Service, Simply Given." The
sacrifice, compassion and generosity of not only the
residents of Moose River but of hundreds of
volunteers, who came from the rest of Nova Scotia
and the Maritimes, has been well documented. Greed
was the cause of the accident. Heroism and rescue
were the results. The heroic actions and
compassionate attitude of the people involved in the
whole tragedy is what has been recorded. In today's
media I cry out for more stories about the positive

side of life. One of my convictions, bolstered by this story is that God does not send fate to rest upon those who tamper with nature in destructive ways. They bring it on themselves; and even a compassionate God cannot intervene and change the course of nature.

The soul of nature is simply that much more powerful than the souls of those individuals who play mischief with nature. At times nature can be cruel indeed. I do believe that collectively we sometimes do serious harm to nature. Yet I also believe that in the Moose River rescue operation, the soul of God was working together with the volunteers in their successful efforts to bring about a rescue. God was working together with the souls of men like Billy Bell and Frank Willis and the women of Moose River who did their part to create good out of tragedy. The Soul of the Universe influenced a man like Billy Bell. Billy was the dedicated operator of the draegermen's diamond drill who insisted that the entombed men were alive while most others had given up hope. He persuaded the engineers who had far more college training than he, to keep on with the rescue. At fourteen years of age I did not have any underlying understanding of how the grace of God, working through people like Billy Bell, would impact my decision to become a minister. Was my soul and the Soul of the Universe already in a meaningful relationship? Four more years on the farm provided opportunities for soul growth before I made a decision to train for the ministry.

Had that soul relationship started long before, when I milked my first cow? My work on the farm, in close touch with the soul of Nature, contributed to my spiritual growth. The weather seems to have been a major factor in the intertwining of my soul with the soul of the natural world. I wonder what the weather will be like on that day when my soul departs to join the Soul of the Universe. As some minister says the words, "ashes to ashes, earth to earth" will the background music be soul friends singing "Up, Up and Away.

Soul Development While Ministering in Boiestown

It is time to reflect on your first career job. This essay may help with your reflections. A well functioning soul is necessary in order to adapt to any sudden radical change in one's journey. I reflect on the change involved in moving from living in uptown Manhattan to the heart of rural New Brunswick.

My wife Lillian and I had been living at Union Theological Seminary in the shadow of Columbia University. I had been invited to assume responsibilities as the newly inducted minister of the Boiestown Pastoral Charge in central New Brunswick. The area was supported by the lumber industry and sports salmon fishing. These four years we were there provided a time for establishing relationships with people who were the salt of the earth. Bonds are still there after many years. It was a time of soul mate bonding with Lillian. We had been married ten months earlier. Her youthfulness was verified by the fact that on more than one occasion a parishioner would knock on the door looking for me and asking Lillian "Is your father home?" Those years provided an opportunity for renewing my bonding with nature. Highlights included a canoe fishing trip Lillian and I made down the famous Miramichi River. Our hosts were Blair Hunter and his wife. Five of us , one of the Hunter's sons and the two couples loaded canoes, grub and gear onto the train and headed to the upper reaches of the Miramichi River where we disembarked at a bridge crossing the river in the midst of nowhere. Our journey back to Boiestown by canoe fulfilled a recurring need of mine for exploration and new experiences. I learned how to pole a canoe, often from a standing position, racing through fast waters and avoiding boulders that could instantly break a canoe into two pieces.

Another image comes forth of an early morning effort at catching the elusive prized salmon. I was fishing in a pool in the river out behind the parsonage where we lived. Wading out into the stream, I hooked into one of my first catches on the river. A saintly elder from my Hayesville congregation was anchored in the far side of the pool. He was the guide for an American tourist who was equally eager to catch a big one. Once I hooked my fish, the elder called across the water "What have you got?" My reply was that it was a grilse, grilse being a small younger salmon. No sooner than my reply had waved itself across the water, my fish leapt out of the water in its effort to free itself, whereupon the saintly man from my congregation in his excitement called back "That ain't no grilse that's a goddamn salmon." It was the language of the river and as comrades and fellow fishermen, there was no requirement for any apology nor even recognition of the use of God's name in vain. We were bonded together and with nature. Few elders and ministers within the structure of today's Church could bond in this fashion. I'm certain that the

Soul of the Universe was smiling in enjoyment of the event.

A soul grows and develops over time. The idea of training volunteers grew out of necessity. Beginning in Boiestown, I provided leadership in developing a volunteer program to assist me in doing work that was related to my responsibilities as a paid professional. I reflect on my ministry in Boiestown. Throughout my professional careers as a minister and as a counsellor I trained volunteers to assist in the work. Now at the end of my career I understand how the concept of training volunteers has influenced me. I developed that first program out of necessity. There were eight separate communities that made up the Boiestown Pastoral Charge. With no competition from television or sports, the people of each community wanted weekly services. During my first year, I was providing four services on Sunday and another on Wednesday night. What to do? With the support of the session, we began a program of selecting lay people, who conducted services while I was busy in another Church. The man who called across the waters "That ain't no grilse that's a goddamn salmon" was a member of that session. One of those trained couples, Claude and Clara Palmer, had a daughter who became an ordained United Church minister. Back then Claudia was a cute little girl with long tresses. Did her parent's involvement in providing those services influence her career decision?

Both laity and minister were empowered through this volunteer program. I utilized the concept in a different way while at the Atlantic Christian Training Centre. I imported the concept into a volunteer program at the North Shore Counselling Centre in West Vancouver. We trained hundreds of volunteers there to provide support for individuals and families who were experiencing stressful times. There were three very important aspects of the training. Do not attempt to do counselling, keep your own problems out of the way and know the difference between empathy and sympathy.

The soul of a whole community can be empowered as well. Boiestown provided an opportunity for finding ways to give the community power for improving its soul. Men from the communities of Boiestown and Bloomfield Ridge took to the woods with their axes and saws and cut logs. The logs were exchanged at a local sawmill for lumber. The lumber was then used by the men, with the help of a few women, to build two outdoor skating rinks. Those who came to help represented the community and not any particular denomination.

Another service which we developed for three of those communities was to provide a movie night. We arranged a long term rental of a projector and screen from the Fredericton branch of the National Film Board of Canada. The branch sent us films for showing on a weekly basis. My task was that of training operators for the projectors. Other people looked after the logistics of that community program. This project got a most positive reception from the community.

The importance of ritual and dignity made an imprint on my professional development while I was in Boiestown. Once a month, a carload of Masons travelled to Fredericton to take part in meetings of the Masonic Lodge. I hardly knew the word Mason other than in the building trade. Impressed by the character of those particular men in my congregation I began to ask questions. I was invited to submit myself to the membership process. I studied and worked through the first three degrees and held an office. I maintained my membership until I left Tatamagouche. Membership standards for entrance were high. The secrecy aspect of the rituals meets some of the little boy's need, still active in grown men. I neither experienced nor witnessed any cult characteristics in the Masonic rituals. Small groups that meet on a regular basis are important for community development. Souls have a role to play in assisting the growth of individuals as they gather in small groups. These small groups are not as structured as the Masonic lodge. Their rituals may include sharing their ideas about a book while enjoying a lunch or a cup of tea. The emergence of the women's movement over the past five decades has contributed to an increase in these groups. Once again community is present as one of the constants of the universe.

Our training for the ministry did not prepare us for every situation when serving rural communities. There were no guidelines set forth in stone for a pastoral care response to the following incidents. One of the prominent families in the congregation had moved their elderly uncle and brother to a nursing home in Miramichi, far down river. His residency there was brief. He died shortly after his arrival at the home. When the undertaker released the body for its return to Boiestown there was not only shock but total denial. Definitely this was not their man; someone had made a grave mistake. The family believed that the undertaker somehow had changed bodies and given them the wrong corpse. The family reluctantly admitted their denial prior to setting the date for the funeral. There was little time since the local undertaker lacked skills in preserving cadavers. Time was of the essence. Occasionally the odour of a decaying corpse added an unpleasant touch to the funeral service. Theological training had not prepared me for managing such crises.

Likewise, newly ordained ministers were not given instructions in proceeding with dignity in all situations. Any theological professor who had never served in a rural parish could not provide instructions to a novice caught in the following situation. One community had been waiting for two years for a pastor who had the credentials to administer the sacraments. Then I arrived. At my first baptism in Holtville there were twelve babies, many of them at the age when they were easily frightened by strangers and loud music. As I sprinkled the now blessed water on the head of the first one in line, the baby sounded the alarm. Eleven other little ones joined the chorus. I was nervous to begin with. Now I was totally confounded. It was only later on reflection that

I recall that all twelve had picked up the same note on the scale of music. Only yesterday, I heard the same musical schematic built into the fabric of nature. A pack of dogs on the make after a bitch in heat picked up the right note when one of their pack sounded the mating chord. The dogs moved on and I returned to enjoying the warm sun and soft breezes of a stress free afternoon walk. Back in that little Holtville Church packed full with people, I wanted to run and leave everything for the two elders to restore order out of chaos.

What might have been fatal to the reputation of the new minister in Boiestown was an incident with a cat. Lillian and I were on our way to some now forgotten Church event down river. In the middle of the Village two cats dashed across the road in front of our car. One very large cat didn't make it. The cat belonged to Mrs. Allen, a kingpin in the Catholic Church. Although my response with the brakes was not good enough, my problem solving skills rapidly came into play. I opened the trunk with the dead cat in hand, threw it in hoping no one witnessed the one-minute crisis and moved on. We later heard about the strange disappearance of the cat. If any descendant of Mrs. Allen by chance reads this page, a longstanding mystery is solved more than sixty years later. Boiestown did not have a crime squad. It did have a communication network through Mrs. Allen's control of the switchboard in a room in her house. Not quite the speed of e-mail but superior beyond any competition in the field of information technology

back in the mid century. The incident with the cat was
locked in a strongbox of secrecy. Only now is the
story being told.

I did not become a soul friend with Mrs. Allen.
Yet I always had respect and gratitude for her
support and contribution to the community and to the
local Catholic Church. Other Catholics I remember
from my association with them include Hedley
McCloskey, with whom I hunted deer and cut logs to
build a local skating rink. Father Wallace and his
attractive housekeeper formed part of my association
with Catholics. We exchanged roles as hosts to each
other. Father Wallace had decided to resolve a
forbidden conflict between spirit and nature. There
was an imbalance between his natural spirit and the
rules of the Church. Eventually nature would have its
way. Father Wallace and the attractive Rita began
sharing the same bed. The unfortunate part was that,
being suspicious, Mrs. Allen went in early one
morning and caught them in bed. Mrs. Allen played a
major role in helping Father Wallace and the Church
to supersede what might have been a scandal. Rita
was dismissed immediately from her position of
housekeeper of the rectory. The whole village knew
and talked for a while. Making it public was part and
parcel of bringing healing to the congregation. Mrs.
Allan had the technology for spreading the news. The
Boiestown folk were people who understood the need
for an appropriate tension between Spirit and nature
in the bedroom. They understood better than the
Fathers of the early Church, who for reasons of

control copied Greek philosophy and created the unnatural division.

There were a few individuals in the Boiestown area who were not members or adherents of my congregations. They were out there on the fringes of my area of pastoral care. Without proselytizing, I would visit people from other denominations occasionally. One of these was Sandy Palmer. Sandy and his wife had separated. He built his cabin at the end of the long lane to the farmhouse where he once lived. There he could watch his wife's comings and goings. Mrs. Palmer remained in the house. On my first visit Sandy explained how his wife had divided the marital home. "She kept the inside and gave me the outside." When Sandy died I administered the usual last rituals in the Bloomfield United Church. The last fifteen minutes of that service turned into somewhat of a chaotic scene. So real was the incident that some congregants were certain that Sandy had been resurrected. His estranged wife was delivered to the funeral by the local Pentecostal minister. She arrived just as the closing hymn was being sung. She stood up to give her prepared speech and lost control. Whereupon she proceeded to the open casket and drew Sandy to her bosom. The local undertaker and I pried her loose and Elbie, the undertaker, escorted her to the door.

Another one of these fringe people was Black Jack MacDonald. He was the local hermit who only emerged from the woods after dark. Occasionally he dropped out of his hiding place to shop at Hunter's store. There he bought a sufficient supply of groceries to last until his next venture out into civilization. It seemed that he had lived in his cabin in the woods for years. Obviously he was a very private person. He communicated very little when I visited him after an intense search to find his place

Bert was another fringe adherent. Bert had a reputation in the Miramichi Valley that focused on his activities while somewhat inebriated. It was my observation that Bert could not help himself. Alcoholics Anonymous might have been the answer. Bert never attained the blissful condition of living as a dry alcoholic. A report that came my way after I left Boiestown brought the news that a car killed him while he was walking on the Fredericton-Miramichi highway.

One Sunday evening Bert came to Church at Bloomfield. The people in the pews turned to see who was coming to Church at the mid-point of the service. Burt, with an unstable walk, made his way to a back pew where teenage boys always sat. The boys were more than amused. They managed to sit uncomfortably through a sermon that now was of little interest to them. After the benediction, Bert remained in his seat while people said their goodbyes. When I approached Bert, he was openly honest about his reason for coming to Church "Would I take him home to Ludlow after the service. I want my wife to see who I have been with." He might have asked any one of the men to be his taxi driver. I agreed to meet his request understanding that he had a good reason for choosing the minister. Bert would have to wait for his ride because I had a commitment to meet with a committee. George Moir, who lived across the way, invited Bert to go across the road and share the warmth of their home. It was a chilly evening. As I approached the house to pick up my passenger I found Mrs. Moir sitting on their verandah. She was either afraid to be in their house with an inebriated individual, or she remained outside simply on principle. On the drive to Bert's residence he implored me to come in and visit his wife, who was ill in bed. Bert was sober enough to carry through on his plan. He told me again how much he wanted his wife to see the minister with whom he had spent the evening. I had decided that I would be a caring soul rather than a self-righteous person. I saw the humour of my predicament and put aside any feelings of resentment that might emerge about getting caught in an alcoholic's way of thinking. I never did discover whether Bert's reputation rose to a new high or whether the minister of the United Church in Boiestown lost considerable prestige for having been out with Bert for the evening.

There were numerous individuals in the congregations who were faithful members of the flock. Most were ordinary, down to earth people whose wisdom had been gained from experience. Some of that wisdom had been passed on to them through generations of their families. One woman who stood out was Rube, partly because she spoke what was on her mind. Another of her traits was that the colour and texture of her hair was the same as that of her pet dog. My first introduction to Rube was when, at the end of my first sermon, she stood up and called to me "John, you done right good."

Lillian and I strayed away from my Pine Hill instructions about not playing favourites in one's congregation. As a young couple arriving in a strange community and ill-prepared for the challenges ahead we needed support. Two families in separate communities included us in such a way that we responded in a soul bonding series of events; those of Gerald and Vivian O'Donnell and Glen and Bertha Green. The experience of bonding with these two families taught us much that became useful in our ministry later in our journey. One such experiential lesson was how to ask for support. Another was the need to learn skills for building a soul-like relationship without neglecting others for whom we were responsible by way of my work.

Another lesson learned very well at the knees of my parents was never to carry stories into these relationships about other people in the community. In my training as a pastoral counsellor, confidentiality was emphasized so intensely that it became part and parcel of the fabric of my being. There is another way of looking at the issue of confidentiality. It is called triangling. Triangling, either in a family or in a small community, is when two members of the family system form two sides of a triangle to talk about real or perceived actions or characteristics of a third

family member. Triangling can make an outcast of a
family member. In a congregation the negative effects
of triangling are far greater than simply being left out.
Whole new denominations have had their original
start by two or three people seeing themselves as
victims and then triangling for support. They see
themselves as victims and they select others as their
enemies. A little congregation on Bowen Island
experienced this twice in a row over a very short span
of time. Their ministers had triangled in destructive
ways. A psychiatrist friend of mine accompanied me
to a service conducted by one of those ministers. His
comment following the service: "John there was a lot
of self-serving going on from the pulpit this
morning."

Two clergy families and one medical family were
outstanding in their support for the young couple
who had come from away to live and work in the
Boiestown area. We had selected Dr Turner in
Fredericton to become our family physician. Dr.
Turner delivered Graeme and Janelle at their birth.
He removed my appendix on a Sunday afternoon in
the old Fredericton hospital, after I had a painful
seizure at the end of the service in Boiestown and was
barely able to pronounce the benediction.

Rev. Roy DeMarsh was my first visitor after the
surgery. I was still heavily sedated. Roy and the
nurses claimed that I entertained them with a speech
that went something like "You can sprinkle them,
dunk them or even drown them for all I care." No
doubt under the influence of the ether, my soul had

made a link with my experience with those twelve babies at the first baptism in Holtville.

Coincidences are sometimes arranged by souls. One such coincidence took place during a visit from Dr. Turner and his wife Dolly. We were at dinner in our Boiestown parsonage. Lillian was wearing a necklace on which dangled an award that I had received when the I was the pope at Pine Hill in Halifax. Pope being the title awarded to the president of the student's council. The award was given in memory of a student who lived at Pine Hill; Graeme Fraser was experimenting in the Chemistry laboratory at Dalhousie when he was killed in an accident. Dolly Turner asked Lillian about the necklace. Drama unfolded as Lillian told her that it had been given to me as an award in memory of Graeme Fraser. Dolly turned white and then a pregnant silence filled the room. Something of a 5.6 magnitude jolt had just occurred. On composing herself Dolly was able to tell us that she had been engaged to Graeme Fraser at the time of his death. Although I had never met Graeme Fraser, a sort of bonding with his soul took place in those moments. Dolly had married Dr. Turner after the death of his first wife.

Another family in Fredericton who became close friends was Dr. George and Mrs. Young and their maiden daughter Helen. Dr. Young was a retired United Church minister whose memory was chock-full of history. He baptized Graeme and Janelle in New Brunswick and came to Tatamagouche to baptize Larry, our third child.

The official announcement of Larry's arrival on
planet earth is of interest. My friend of Dalhousie
days Dr Austin Creighton delivered Larry in the
cottage hospital in Tatamagouche. Austin and I
developed a soul friend relationship during the ten
years we lived in Tatamagouche. We had lived
together at Pine Hill for a number of years earlier. In
his mischievous way he called me immediately after
Larry's arrival to announce that I was the father to
two boys. Recovering from the shock I gradually
realized that one of those boys was Larry's older
brother Graeme.

In reaching out to play, my soul easily found a
comfortable place in nature. This was particularly
true while we lived both in Boiestown and later in
Nashwaaksis. Hunting partridge and deer, although
seasonal, competed for time at work and with the
family. In the early days Lillian went with me when I
hunted partridge. Men from the community and the
congregation became my outdoor pals in both the
Miramichi valley and the Saint John River valley. My
bonding with nature back in those areas of New
Brunswick was so cemented that I returned there to
hunt and fish several times after we moved to
Tatamagouche.

I still go back to Boiestown occasionally to canoe
down the river from Hayesville at the upper end of
the pastoral charge to Ludlow or Doaktown. On one
of these forages back to nature I stayed overnight in
an upscale fishing lodge in Ludlow. My soul rejoiced
as it was nurtured with reflections and memories of a

distant past. I was blessed with having a wonderful companion with whom I could share both present and past. When we lived in the area, only the rich American fishermen and hunters could afford the luxury of that lodge. On this occasion I was rich in more ways than one.

The young minister who grew up in the Musquodoboit valley came to the Miramichi without ever having connected with rich people. Putting it mildly I was intimidated in their presence. Not because of their attitude but because of my own lack of experience with money folk. Those special tourists returned again and again to the area. They knew how to relate to the guides, their families, and locals. When we built a new Church hall at Bloomfield Ridge a number of the rich Americans donated to the cause. Naturally I was impressed and grateful.

During those four years at Boiestown, I had no understanding about the meaning of soul. I would have read scripture passages about the soul for the benefit of the congregation. The word would be common in a few hymns. Souls were there at every gathering, their presence ignored, except when some caring person would provide a friendly 'bless your soul'. It was only on reading O'Donohue's book *Anam Cara*, that I began to think about what is meant by soul, a familiar word in many cultures.

Soul Building Is Elusive In the Making of a New Entity

If you have experienced moving from a rural community to a town or city where you hardly know other people on the street, you will resonate with aspects of this essay. How does one find the soul of that community? As an identifiable community it may not have developed a soul.

One wonders how long it takes for the new arrangement of a group of people to develop its own soul. The time involved and the eventual success depend on the ability of people to adjust to change. The adjustment has more to do with letting go of the past than it has with adjusting to the new. By the time I was invited to be the minister of the new entity known as the Nashwaaksis Pastoral Charge, some of the letting go process was in progress. The hub of the new venture, Nashwaaksis, was already experiencing growth as a community. The other two communities that were to be part of this new entity were rural in nature.

The soul of the United Church community in New Maryland across the Saint John river tended to maintain its own identity. Seventy-five percent was rural, with small farms. Geographically, this community was separated from Nashwaaksis by the city of Fredericton and the Saint John River. The community of Mouth of Keswick was up the river and was a farming area. Nashwaaksis had already experienced considerable change, going from a farming community toward becoming a suburb of Fredericton. There were a few men and women who were actively involved in establishing a new vision for the future of Nashwaaksis itself. They were known as town planners. The planners whom I knew had a good sense of blending past with future growth.

Since we moved to Nashwaaksis to take up the task of ministering to people in three diverse communities, the farmland has been turned into developments around the hub of Fredericton, New Brunswick. Part of my new responsibilities was to attempt to merge these entities into a pastoral charge of the United Church of Canada. The attempts at building the larger pastoral charge were unsuccessful. The larger area did not develop a soul of its own in the Irish concept of a community that has a soul. Nashwaaksis as a community already had a recognizable soul.

The following pages record a few accounts of the beginning of the soul building of the congregation known as the Nashwaaksis United Church. From time to time I return there either to worship, or simply to enter the new Church, sit in a pew to reflect, and talk to anyone who has an ear to hear about the old days.

A critical turning point away from the old to the new entity happened at one special meeting of the Church congregation. The congregation would discuss the ideal location for a new Church. The old

Church and the Church hall were bulging at the seams. Church services were crammed with worshippers, requiring chairs for people to sit in the aisles. An active Church school, a new Youth group, and a new Men's group were signals that the time to build or enlarge was upon us.

Families who had been involved in the old Church had memories that were bolstered by strong emotions. They, their children and grandchildren had been baptized in the old Church building. Rites for marriage and funerals of loved ones had been performed in that same old building. There was one family in particular that represented this group of born-here people. That was the Lloyd Johnston family, in which Lloyd was the proponent for hanging onto the old. Lloyd had also been a key player in the activities and business matters of the Church for years.

He and his wife Helen were definitely opposed to building a new Church anywhere except on the present property. It seemed that lines had been drawn in the sand between those who wanted to stay, and those who saw the need for a larger piece of property.

I came to minister among them with no training or experience in conflict resolution. As their leader I was concerned about what would happen at the appointed meeting. I recall two things about my involvement. In a prayer I called upon God to guide us through the process. Looking back, I identify another important aspect of my involvement. I kept quiet and did not interfere with the process. I understood the need for moving on, and I saw the obstacles in the way of expanding the present property. During the meeting, both Helen and Lloyd Johnson spoke strongly and with emotion setting forth their reasons for hanging on to the past by building on the property where we now sat.

Eventually there was a vote which went strongly in favor of finding a new location. Following the vote Lloyd stood up to state, "Helen and I talked at length this past week about the purpose of this meeting. Our sense was that the vote just completed would be in favor of moving. We decided together that if the vote went as it has we want to donate the property for the new Church. We have the property where the old farm once stood. We want to be a part of the change." The soul of this new entity moved those of us who were there. I was filled with joy, augmented by surprise. The soul of the Nashwaaksis United Church had taken on a much larger dimension.

In the summer of 1955 our growing family of Lillian, Graeme and now Janelle moved on to my new career in Tatamagouche. I would be involved in the beginning of a much newer entity: the Atlantic Christian Training Centre. Prior to leaving my ministry at Nashwaaksis, the board of the Church had set up a process for raising funds to purchase a property and build a new Church building. Plans were under way to purchase a property on the Main Street. Lloyd and Helen Johnston's souls were sufficiently big and beautiful to recognize the importance of the selection. The Church would be built on the same street where their store and house were located. Fifty years later it appears that the selection was the right one. I was invited to return to lay the cornerstone for the new Church. Since then, an addition became necessary and was successfully implemented. I looked for the old cornerstone in vain. It seems that it was incorporated into the foundation of the addition.

There were many beautiful souls living across that scattered pastoral charge. I find it difficult to remember any murky souls. It could be that had we stayed more than three years, one or two murky souls would have emerged from the darkness.

I'll introduce you to three of those beautiful souls. Only one of these merged sufficiently with my soul to claim that we became soul friends. Otis Currie was a fundamentalist Baptist brought up in a semi-fundamentalist tradition. His soul was sufficiently open that he was comfortable in our United Church, and he became an important member of the Church session. Otis was a trainman who worked on the railroad. One of his tasks was to carry the warning lantern on the last car of the train. Today that service is provided by a black box positioned at the end of the train.

Otis had considerable skills as a carpenter. I joined him in building an office desk for the Church. The production was an attractive and useful piece of furniture. We began work on a similar desk for my office in Tatamagouche. When it was finished, Otis brought it to Tatamagouche. As I write in West

Vancouver I am sitting at that oak desk. When I work
at my business, or at my computer sitting at that oak
desk, I occasionally remember with delight my
relationship with Otis. Years later I visited Otis and
Betty in their retirement home in Nashwaaksis. Word
about the outbreak of AIDS was just now being
spread. Otis wanted to discuss theology with me. He
reached back into his fundamentalist upbringing and
was convinced that AIDS was God's punishment. The
crime was quite specific. Gay people were being
punished. There was no room or compassion from the
Soul of God for their sin.

About two years after this visit, Otis came into
their home from working his vegetable garden, not
knowing who he was. He never fully recovered his
identity. It was as though he had suddenly developed
a full blown case of the Alzheimer disease. The
medical professionals mistakenly diagnosed Otis as
having cancer and treated him accordingly. In fact
Otis had a stroke that impaired a significant part of
his brain. I visited him in a nursing home about a year
later. He had been treated for months in the
Fredericton hospital for cancer. In talking to Otis, I
remembered our working together building those
desks. Out of that discussion he was able to recall that
John Stewart was his minister. Then he went on to
talk about what a wonderful minister he was. How
fortunate the community was to have him as a
minister. Of interest to me was how Otis talked to me
as though he was sharing his memories with a third
party. I believe that our souls made a significant

connection during that visit. This incident raises issues about souls connecting in the afterlife. By what process were our two souls able to connect while Otis knew neither his own identity, nor the identity of the person sitting with him?

There were two other individuals who surface in my memory, Robin and Jean Holyoke. Robin had a career with a supply company in Fredericton. Each of these individuals became important to the growth of the new congregation. They became friends of Lillian and me during our three years in the community. I have returned to visit them on occasion over the years. Robin and Jean Holyoke were about our age. Robin assisted me in organizing a men's archery group. A number of us purchased bows and arrows. We set up a shooting range with bales of hay for a back-stop. My experience in that group prepared me for hunting rabbits with a bow in Tatamagouche a few years later.

My eldest grandson, two generations later, hunts bear and deer with a crossbow. In the fall of 2006 he set up bait to attract the bear at night. He bought an infra-red camera and got pictures of the bear. One picture shows the bear reaching up to smash the camera from the tree to which it was attached. One evening Micah got a shot at the bear but the arrow did not hit a vulnerable spot. The bear simply reached around to his hip, pulled the arrow out and wandered off.

Jean Holyoke is now a widow, Robin having died after a three year battle with Alzheimer's disease. Jean

and Lillian worked together in their joint leadership
of a teen-age girl's group, CGIT (Canadian Girls in
Training). I have maintained a relationship with Jean
partly due to my memory of stories about her
childhood. Jean grew up in a family that managed a
municipal home for old and handicapped people. It
was known as the Poor Farm. It was the responsibility
of the Municipality. The Currie family, Jean's Mom,
Dad and sister, were tireless workers in the Church
during our three years in Nashwaaksis. Residents of
the Home attended Church regularly. There has been
change. In place of the Poor Farm there is now in
Nashwaaksis a three story residence that provides
home care for the elderly and handicapped people. If
you can afford it, the cost is approximately thirty-five
hundred dollars a month. There is a provincial
subsidy for those who are fortunate enough to get a
space but cannot afford the cost.

In the summer of 2006 I went to the new home to
visit Vivian O'Donnell, the widow of my soul friend
Gerald with whom I bonded in a relationship in
Boiestown. I arrived mid-afternoon to visit Vivian.
My host insisted that she take me to supper in the
community dining hall. The staff was informed. They
set up a special table for us with a candle burning in
the midst of a centre-piece of flowers. We were served
in style as thought we were a bride and groom. I
noted, while we waited for supper that about seventy
five per cent of the residents used wheel-chairs or
walkers. What a creative atmosphere in which to
spend your last years. A caring staff would bring you

from your room to the elevator and wheel you to a table for a good meal. Jean Currie's Mom and Dad did not have such a great setting in which to exercise their compassion and caring. Residents of the Poor Farm filled two pews in our little Church each Sabbath. The compassion of the people in that congregation will have contributed to the change for the better that I witnessed several years later.

As an aside, the Nashwaaksis congregation sold the old Church to the Catholics. It caught fire later and burned to the ground. The cause of the fire was never reported to me, which leaves me to surmise that the fire was started by friction from an unresolved conflict within the soul of the new group housed in an old Protestant building.

To summarize: the United Churches in the three distinct communities of Nashwaaksis, New Maryland and Keswick had been brought together by the action of the Fredericton presbytery to form a new pastoral charge. My attempts to put the plan in action were unsuccessful. No new soul emerged. They were three quite different congregations. Reflection informs me that Nashwaaksis had already become a bedroom community on the outskirts of Fredericton, while the other two were still farming communities. The seeds for soul building were not there. It takes both commonalities and disparities to build a new soul entity.

The soul of the Nashwaaksis congregation flourished. It is now one of the stronger congregations

in a national Church that is closing church buildings
at the rate of one a week.

Parish, Graduate Studies and the Family

The energy it took this afternoon just to keep focused on one simple task of cutting a matting for a picture and putting the picture in a homemade frame was a reminder that I do not have the ability to juggle several balls at one time. I had that skill during the years between 1965 and 1972. When reflecting on filling three major roles for seven years while living in Annisquam provides a clear message that my brain, at age eighty-five, operates at a much slower pace. I am amazed that between the ages of forty-three and fifty one person could function creatively while multi-tasking several major roles. I was father to three growing children and husband to a woman who worked full-time for most of those seven years. I worked on a half-time basis as the pastor of the Annisquam Village Church. I was a full-time student in post graduate work. I worked part-time for three years in a family therapy centre in Gloucester. I served on an internship at the Danielsen Pastoral Counseling Center at Boston University. I participated for one term in a consulting program at the Danielsen Center. I interned for three months in a psychiatric hospital at Danvers. A few of these programs came into place after the completion of one of the others. Back then I was able to juggle several responsibilities at the same time. I wonder now how I was able to be creative through it all. My soul is richer by far, and my wisdom has expanded twofold over the intervening years.

It takes longer now for me to process information. I find myself needing more time to think and to remember. A momentary interruption while I am in the midst of a task is like being away from it for a week. Doing payroll for workers at tree harvest time is a chore that I do not like. Preparing three sets of income taxes has become a challenge. While coping with all the passwords and identities required by computer work, I become muddled at times. Internet banking is part of an overload problem. The problem is more than just growing older. The fast pace of our current culture negates the advantages provided by our high-tech environment. I wonder at times if Bill Gates, and others who have designed programs which overwhelm me, will become senile when they have run out of challenges. If by some fluke you, Bill, should ever read these words, do get in touch and we shall compare. The burden can be overwhelming at times, but there is little doubt that the challenges help to keep me younger.

The responsibilities of being a family man, a parish minister and a graduate student remained throughout the seven years while at Annisquam. It was important to keep the three areas of those responsibilities in balance.

I reflect on my graduate studies. Two clear pictures emerge. The academic studies involved lectures, books, journals and research. The practical requirements provided opportunities to work directly with people. The university had a counselling centre that served a twofold purpose as a service to the community and an experience for the interns. There is no parchment on the wall of my office as proof of that practical experience. I came away from Boston University with an enriched soul impacted by the practical experiences. The reading and lectures expanded my knowledge.

My soul is enriched by sound theology. I was exposed to several counselling theories that have different approaches to people's problems. The combination of theology and counselling theories gave me confidence and expertise for helping clients. The theology and counselling theories were enriched by what I learned from my parishioners, from my fellow students at Boston University, from my work experience at the Cape Ann Children and Family Center, and from my family. My family consisted of Lillian my wife, Graeme our elder son, Janelle our daughter and Larry our younger son. Each one was growing along with me. Their experiences were different: Lillian's at work and the children's at school with their Annisquam friends.

Those six years were the most creative period along my journey. Was it good mental health that kept it all together? Or was the success of that creativity the result of a lively and growing soul that was made richer by other souls? I've concluded that one of the functions of the soul is precisely that, of helping to "keep it all together."

The soul of the family functioned well during this period. Picture a family of five hauling a U-Haul trailer behind the car, heading out into an unpredictable future. Loaded in the trailer were the worldly goods we were going to need when we moved into the parsonage of the Annisquam Church. As we rode along the Trans-Canada heading for the U. S. border, Dad almost lost the works as we descended a long hill. The weight of the goods in the trailer was out of balance, a reminder about the importance of maintaining a proper balance over one's journey.

Before setting out for Boston we had been in transition for two months after leaving the Atlantic Christian Training Centre in Tatamagouche. I had accepted a teaching position for the summer school at Pine Hill Divinity Hall. That was creative for us all. We have a picture of Graeme cruising in our motor boat alongside the Bluenose sailing ship, heading up the Northwest Arm in Halifax. It was a time for remembering and reflecting for me. I enjoyed the honour that was mine in being appointed to the position at Pine Hill. Following the Summer term there, we lived in Lawrencetown, Nova Scotia. In Lawrencetown, I filled the position of supply minister for the month of August. There were limited responsibilities apart from the Sunday services. As a family we were able to explore the Annapolis Valley and the Southern end of Nova Scotia.

Heading for Boston in September we travelled down the Maine turnpike, looking forward to getting settled. The children would be going to schools that were larger than any they had known. Lillian would be looking for work to help with financing the venture. All in all, the venture metamorphosed into an adventure. The three children, ages from nine to fourteen, became preacher's kids for the second time. The expectations from the Annisquam Village Church were not demanding on either Lillian or the children, as they had been at Boiestown and Nashwaaksis.

The differences in the school system created some initial pressure on the children. Graeme needed to do some catching up in Math. Larry seized the opportunity to join a baseball team. Larry also took up golf before we finished our adventure in MA. All three children and I took to downhill skiing. I started a youth group at the Village Church. Creative and industrious lay leaders organized a group ski trip to Stowe in New Hampshire. We skied with the Kennedy family. We recognized them on the chairs ahead of us. We were so enamored by the success of our life together that we wondered why the Kennedy family failed to recognize us. A few years later our family had a similar experience when in line at a chair lift at Whistler in British Columbia. Canadian prime minister Pierre Trudeau was directly in front of us, for another run down the slopes.

Family parties in the homes of two musical families in Annisquam contributed much to the soul of our family. The Dykemans had no children of their own. Myrtle Dykeman gave Larry lessons in the mandolin. Wendell was known as the merry mortician, due to a combination of his profession and his love for table games. The Knowlton family was another family, all of whom were blessed with a love for music. Leah was the choir director at the Church. Their son Jimmy came with us on one of our many motor trips back to Nova Scotia. It was on one of these journeys back to Nova Scotia when I banged up my knee while skiing at Wentworth.

Lillian's sense of self-worth reached an all time high as she was adored by several men in the congregation. Sam Haines, Stan Russell and Sanford Aberle were three of her admirers. Fortunately the wives of each were secure, loving women who had no objections. Jealousy was inoperative because they had no fear of losing their husbands to the minister's wife. An additional bonus for Lillian was that she was not expected to be a contributing member of the Church staff without pay. That expectat5ion was normal in my previous congregations.

There seemed to be few stressors on the family during these six years of intense living. Driving the forty miles to and from Boston in the heat of the Summer is remembered as the hardest part for me. I reflect back on one hot Summer day. Arriving home hot and tired I complained to Janelle about some now long forgotten issue. With most of the windows of the parsonage wide open, and neighboring houses practically butting against ours, Janelle knew what she was up to when she shouted to me at the top of her voice. "You bastard." At the tender age of fifteen Janelle had learned that my favourite swear word was the one she chose at that moment. I waited for the meeting of the personnel committee of the Church board that never happened. To this day Janelle, in her strength as a woman seizes the opportunity every few years to tear a strip off her Dad. Offsetting the hurt is my pride in having such a strong daughter. Graeme and Larry have chosen less public environments to express their frustrations with their Dad.

The children's souls were not connected to my academic life at Boston University. The children's experiences developed with their involvement in their schools, the Church, and the community of Annisquam. Lillian was more involved with the academic side of my life for two reasons which we shall learn about later.

My Soul and the Annisquam Village Church

I reflect on my soul's involvement with the congregation of the Church. Every Sunday morning the number of souls in attendance was posted in the vestibule. The Annisquam Village Church was open to experimentation, especially in the field of music. It was and is a Church where, with dignity, there is a balance between the old and the new. For our three children it was a significant part of their lives. They along with their parents and the congregation sang with joy 'Up, Up and Away' as children released balloons at the annual outdoor Easter morning service at Squam Rock.

Yes, I cried at my daughter Janelle's wedding, which I conducted when we went back to the Village Church for her marriage to Neal in 1975. They were tears of joy for Janelle that were mixed with feeling lonesome for Graeme, who could not be there for the ceremony. After a couple of deep breaths, I was able to proceed with certainty and a calmness appropriate for the occasion.

The simple beauty of the Church sanctuary created a worshipful atmosphere as soon as your soul entered its interior. I assume that the serenity persisted when the only occupants were souls from the past. For that reason, the doors were never locked during my six years there. One can best describe it as holy beauty. The setting of the Church building is also inspiring. It is located at the head of the Cove where the tide comes and goes, twice in twenty four hours, reminding us of the constancy of God's love and care. Between my study window and the cove there was a beautiful New England style home. The music for the Sound of Music was written in that house. The property remained in the hands of a woman who was closely connected with Richard Rodgers of Rodgers and Hammerstein. What a setting for preparing the sermon for Sunday.

The whole population of Annisquam were part and parcel of my pastorate. In their midst, I, along with my family, was accepted as one of them. The makeup of the congregation was emblematic of the cultural essence of the wider community. There were the old Annisquam families, many of them had wealth. Yet for the most part, these families never made a display of their wealth. I remember Paul and Isobel Sargent and their neighbours Charlie and Bertha Heberle. All of them were down to earth folk. On a Saturday one could meet Paul either in his old car, or walking about dressed as one of my workers at tree harvest time. Then, there were the "nouveau riche" who had not as yet learned how to be comfortable with their wealth. That takes time for most souls. Sudden increase in wealth is not always good for the soul. Reinhold Niebuhr, an able theologian at Union Seminary, claimed in a class on ethics that "pride, not money, is the root of all evil." In addition we had among us, both in the Church and out there in the wider community, those families who from time to time were recognized in their need. They

warranted some financial assistance from the
minister's discretionary fund.

Sunday services and pastoral care were the
responsibilities outlined in my contract with the
Church. Due to my program at Boston University I
would at times take on a counselling case from the
community rather than refer the person on to a
professional. My usual custom was to refer. Two or
three situations are significant. I met a few times with
a couple, one of whom was quite depressed. One
symptom of the depression was the emergence of
paranoid notions. It was my first introduction to how
one person's fantasies and paranoia can spread to a
whole neighborhood. Quite a few people in the
neighborhood began to believe that the mafia had
invaded the community. The paranoia started with
my client. We have witnessed how this works when a
few associates of President Bush became paranoid
about Iraq, and a very large segment of the American
population was vulnerable to what may have begun
with one person's paranoia.

One individual was referred to me because he
had some strange ideas. A few minutes into our
session he claimed that he was Thor, the
Scandinavian God. Not knowing just how to respond
to his fantasies, I decided that the wisest way was to
go along with him and be a listening supporter. A
week later I presented the case to my supervisor at
Boston University. I felt affirmed when he told me
that my response was a most professional one. He
indicated that to try to talk the client out of his

fantasies would simply convert me from a supportive listener to become one of the people about who the client was paranoid. A great lesson learned.

Two instances of pastoral care work serve to illustrate the vulnerability of being a minister. Both had to do with couples. One wife approached me indicating that she was being physically abused. I met with her and her husband on a one time basis, and came to the conclusion that the situation had not approached the crisis stage. However I did give them advice about steps they could take if either of them became concerned about further developments. Shortly after this she decided to remove herself from the relationship. Then for months after our session, every time the husband and I met on the narrow highway between Annisquam and Gloucester he would swerve his car toward mine, making as though he would run me down. I did not flinch nor did I report him to the police. After a time he decided that his game was not working.

A one-time counselling session with another couple had a curious outcome. As I learned later from the wife she was the one who instigated the counselling session. Months later, one winter evening she walked into my office at the Church where I was working. She told me that she had come many times and parked across the street watching my window. Finally she gained sufficient courage to approach me . Her purpose, as she announced, was that she wanted to have an affair with me. By this time, my training was sufficiently polished that I responded with care. I explained that I was her minister and that I was a married man with a family. Rather than scold her for her interest, I simply denied her request. It was sufficient to explain to her the reality of my family and pastoral circumstances. The next week, I presented this situation to my supervisor, who affirmed the caring manner in which I responded. Three years later, on one of my visits back from Canada to Annisquam, her husband asked to meet with me. He wanted to check out what his wife had told him in one of their fights. She told him that I had promised her that I would return from Canada and take her back to Canada with me. Would I simply deny her claim or would I report to him how she had come to me asking for sexual involvement? Would I tell him about my response and how it was affirmed by a supervisor? I choose simply to deny her claim, and to assure him that I had only one brief meeting with her in the Church office. I had no need to get caught in a triangle with this couple by joining their fight. My pastoral care does not include tattling on a parishioner indiscretion.

Some couples have a tendency of solving their issues by turning on their therapist. They stop seeing their partner as the enemy; they join hands and make the helper the enemy. Watch out you volunteer helpers and friends of spouses who turn to you for a shoulder to cry on. Friends and parents of those couples who are going through separation beware. Your good intentions in giving advice sometimes help to line the pockets of lawyers. If you were required to pay the legal fees, your support would be less destructive. It is always easy to offer advice to others to spend money foolishly, so long as it is not your money.

It was the first week of July in 1972 when I rented a Ford U-Haul truck in Boston. We loaded it with our goods and headed for the West Coast of Canada. Our relationship with the soul of the Annisquam community could not be terminated so easily. Three different families have come to visit us on the West Coast. Members of the Juncker family still come to visit with us in West Vancouver. Each member of our family has gone back to connect and to renew. My Christmas tree career has provided opportunities to return to Annisquam. A number of the people with whom I had a close relationship have died. One of my close friends Isobel Sargent said to me on my last visit with her "John, growing old is no fun. The quality of my days is like the tide in the Cove below our garden. The tide comes and goes." Will Isobel and I meet again through the medium of our souls?

Moving on to new adventures seems to be a common theme in the journey of my soul. Are you who reads these pages prepared for the great unknown adventure? Will the final adventure be the realization of the prayer of my childhood "If I should die before I wake I pray the Lord my soul do take?"

Transcontinental Career Change

Picture yourself sitting behind the wheel of a large Ford van on the Massachusetts turnpike. Your younger son and your wife are driving behind in the family car. You are about a hundred miles along the first leg of a three thousand mile journey from Annisquam, Massachusetts to Vancouver, British Columbia. Having gained confidence in driving the big moving van, your thoughts change to the significance of your career change. Suddenly you realize that you have lost contact with your spouse and younger son. In the excitement of pulling up roots in Annisquam we failed to plan for any such contingency. It is near noon and there will be no contact until the next morning. Lillian and Larry, along with the family cat, were on their own. Finding it difficult to drive behind the van, Lillian decided to move up front. Unfortunately the cell phone had not been invented and we lost contact for twenty four hours. Musing about the impact on my soul due to my career change would have to wait.

Shortly after Lillian made her decision to move ahead, the Ford U-haul balked and suddenly quit. Stalling every hundred miles on average, was to be the pattern all the way to Regina. Prior to Regina, the only solution I knew to get going again was to wait a bit for the engine to cool. I would go and find some fresh gas. The cold gas served as a tonic for the engine. U-Haul experts at their Canadian headquarters in Hamilton, Ontario were unable to fix the problem; even with a new carburetor. A wise mechanic in a little garage on the outskirts of a Prairie town suggested that I carry along a pail of water and apply a wet cloth to the gas line at the point where the line crossed the exhaust pipe. Eureka!

That day on the New York turnpike I reported to the police that I had lost my wife and son. The police failed in their attempts to reunite us. I kept moving on, keeping with the plan we had made to stop that night with Lillian's sister and family in Hamilton, Ontario. I expected to find a message from Lillian when I reached Hamilton. There was no message. Lillian and Larry stopped for the night in a motel in Rochester. She didn't call until the next morning when she reached the border at Niagara Falls. The customs officer wanted certain documents which I had with me. We were united at the Canadian customs office in Niagara a few hours later.

On arrival in Hamilton we found ourselves back in our homeland. This journey had started in Nova Scotia. Just prior to loading the van in Annisquam I had gone to Nova Scotia and hired a trailer to add belongings to our Annisquam possessions.

Bob Collings came along as far as Winnipeg to help with the driving. Graeme came from Kimberley in British Columbia to Calgary to meet us. Graeme was working at a mine in Kimberley to earn money to return to Simon Fraser University in September. He came to assist his dad with the driving through the Alberta and British Columbia mountains.

The journey across the continent was smooth and enjoyable apart from the two problems already recorded. Driving through the mountains was a challenge. We still needed our towel and a pail of water to cool the gasoline.

Graeme had been in British Columbia for a year where he attended Simon Fraser University. He worked during the Summer at a smelter in Kimberley. Prior to our arrival he had arranged for us to rent a house in the British Properties in West Vancouver. The Jaffrey family consisting of mom, dad and two teenage daughters were going to France for a year. What a break for us in being able to rent a furnished house. Graeme was already doing his second stint at parenting his parents. We knew that we needed a year to make a decision about buying a house in the community where I was to begin my new career.

We stayed the first night in a downtrodden motel in North Vancouver, before we could move into that rather pleasing open-beam house. The Jaffrey house was located in the wealthiest area of West Vancouver, the British Properties. The story about the Properties is that the Guinness family built the Lions Gate Bridge to connect the North Shore with Vancouver. In exchange for the bridge they were given a large grant of property on the foothills of Cypress Mountain. Houses here have increased in value more than fifteen-fold since our arrival.

In our previous moves, we had gained some expertise in getting to know the people of our community. We hosted several parties in the Jaffrey house as a way of getting acquainted with members of the board of the centre where I worked. The wife of one guest refused to attend one of our parties. Her husband came anyway and explained that she did not want to meet up with two of the guests who would be there. Her neighbours had a large dog that had recently eaten her little poodle. Her husband, our guest, was a very open person. He quietly explained his wife's absence. I noted that he engaged freely with the owners of the monster dog. Jim's soul was not going to be tarnished by a dog fight.

Recalling this event reminds me of our experience when we first moved to Boiestown, New Brunswick. I ran over Mrs. Allen's cat. The night was dark so I stopped and dumped the cat in the trunk of the car and moved on. If I had to do it over again would I go and apologize to Mrs. Allen? Fortunately there never was a public inquiry over the missing cat. A call to be a witness might have abruptly ended my ministry in Boiestown.

It is nearly four decades since we made that trip across the continent. It's the middle of April and Spring has arrived here in West Vancouver. Our experience over the last thirty-five years confirms that global warming is a reality. That winter back in 1971, I had to shovel the snow off the roof of the Jaffray house for fear of it collapsing under the weight. In 1972 I returned to the East for an event. I arrived back in West Vancouver in time for Mother's Day. After attending church, I drove up to the top of the British Properties to see how many inches of snow had fallen over the night. There has been only one winter since when we have experienced such a major snow storm in West Vancouver.

Every year since my retirement in 1987 I have enjoyed two Spring seasons. Now in mid-April, I'm looking forward to my second Spring in Nova Scotia. The lilacs bloom in early May in West Vancouver. I have seen lilac bushes come into bloom in July on the Eastern shores of Nova Scotia. Has global warming changed the season's pattern in Ecum Secum by now?

The ice melting in the waters on Canada's North Coast is producing noticeable changes. Warm air currents are pushing cold air down into the central parts of North America while temperatures in Iqaluit are warmer some days than they are in Fredericton.

Like the weather, our family was experiencing major changes. With these big changes our souls would have work to do as we established new identities building upon the old. New surroundings, new homes, new schools, new careers and new friendships would require significant adjustments.

Janelle our daughter made her trip across the continent later in the summer. With her boyfriend Neal they would begin their first year in university at Simon Fraser University in Burnaby, a suburb of Vancouver. Larry would choose which of the local high schools he would attend.

Not a single one of us would have time for reflection. At this point in time the soul of our family was at risk. Never before was there such a need for us as a family to reflect on our past in order to be better prepared for the near term future. Our souls would be on their own. Without time for reflection, we were unaware of where we would be going.

Soul Expands In Making a New Entity

From an early age you will have had an inborn tendency to create and build new things. Your curiosity would have been a key factor in forming ideas and building things that had not been part of your life previously. Was your soul functioning in tandem with that curiosity? Was your creativity supported by other saintly souls or impeded by murky souls? To what extent did parents and babysitters encourage your curiosity?

The fifteen years' of building what became known as the North Shore Counselling Centre cover a period of rich growth for my soul. More than one hundred people in the West Vancouver United Church community had a vision. Back in 1971 it became my task of carrying their vision forward. With the help of dedicated individuals we not only nourished and maintained their vision, we enlarged it at a rate that was manageable. I was grateful for the skills in administration that I had learned at Tatamagouche. For the first few years, our budget in West Vancouver was doubling annually. There were individuals like Norman Alban and Russell Kinnemont who helped us to stay on track financially. In that area we differed from the Pastoral Institute in Vancouver which eventually went bankrupt. My first love was not in administration. My greatest personal satisfaction came from the counselling and from training volunteers. My gift as an administrator was my ability to develop a vision and to be realistic when carrying it onward. Several years after my retirement I was with Don McLean at a public meeting when he told the group that he admired my ability to have a vision for the Centre. A number of us who attended that same meeting stood for our vision. The outcome being that the group voted to stay on course. The purpose of that meeting was to make a decision about whether or not to accept the offer of the Family Services of the North Shore to acquire the Centre. I believed that with good administration, the Centre would correct its financial difficulties. The soul of the Family Services group had a murky side, reflected in jealousy. Obviously I was delighted with the outcome of the meeting. The Family Services agency did not succeed in taking over the project we had begun back in 1971. I hope to live to be one hundred so, in another few years, I can be around for the 50th anniversary of the Centre.

My basic academic training in counselling happened at Boston University. My training was grounded in two theories. Psychotherapy and developmental theory melded into each other as I took courses at the University. My three years of experience as an intern at the Danielsen Pastoral Counseling Centre in Boston was the frosting on the cake in comparison with the academic courses.

Two cases serve as classic for illustrating each of the two theories.

Developmental theory was my model when helping one man I will call Cedric, for the sake of his privacy. Cedric was a man of thirty-five who was not making any headway in either his career nor in his interpersonal relationships. At an early age he was a latch-key child in New York city. Both parents were at work. He wore a latch-key around his neck in order to gain entrance to his home. His first breakthrough in therapy came as he talked about a personal crisis. Cedric was on his way home from school. On arriving at their house he could not find his key. He had two friends with him. The crisis was that he needed to get to the bathroom. His only choice now was to let it all go in his pants. As I listened to Cedric's story, and observed how distraught he was in the here and now, the room filled with a most obnoxious odour. Cedric was reliving his crisis. Only this time his anal expulsions were limited to several loud farts. In the here and now Cedric cried a bit. He was surprised that I appeared to be not at all embarrassed. So why should he?

Cedric was ready to move forward in his therapy. In a session some weeks later he talked about his relationship with his mother. He recalled being in the garden one sunny day with his Mom. His memory was conflicted by feelings of guilt as he saw his mother's breasts. He saw them as big tomatoes which he wanted to pick and hold. Cedric had not moved out of that stage of childhood where such a fantasy would be normal. He was stuck back in a childhood stage of development. His sharing of the experience helped him to skip more than a dozen years of development. Cedric reported later that he now enjoys breasts as part of normal sexual activity.

I find it difficult to imagine myself being stuck back there in the face of current fashion. I have noted with enjoyment how some women wear blouses which expose most of their breasts. In this day and age of political correctness, is a man not supposed to look? Women in two separate offices in Truro, Nova Scotia solve that problem for me. They sit at their desk directly in front of where I am standing. There is a low counter between us. We are almost face to face. This provides the opportunity to look at both their face and breasts in one fell swoop. I wish I had more excuses to return to their desks for additional help. The women know and I know that our souls have met, but momentarily. Where is the Soul of the Universe at those moments? It is not politically correct to verbalize what we both know. I say nothing and they will continue to wear seductive blouses.

Stages of development fade into the background a bit during the years of twenty to forty. They emerge with new energy in the late thirties and onward into the sixties. Yet the soul develops all along the way, building a foundation for getting to know where you are going once you reach middle age. Knowing where you have been helps in preparing oneself for growing old.

I remember well the case of one woman who was forty-nine when she began her therapy. Susan talked about her anger over two different men who had taken advantage of her financially. As her counsellor I

began to sense that finding the right man was one
way of avoiding facing that she was growing older
and had not even considered that one day she would
die. Susan had neglected to feed her soul. I worked
with Susan within a framework of psychotherapy. In
our sessions together we were making a bit of
progress, slowly but surely. One day she came into
the session looking troubled. As soon as she sat down
in a comfortable chair she began to cry, sobbing
loudly. When she settled down I remarked "Would
you like to tell me what is troubling you Susan? With
a body stance that showed fear, she replied "It is my
birthday and I'm half a hundred." My response
turned out to be one of the best of my counselling
career. "Susan, you are only twice twenty-five." This
was the beginning of serious work both in the
sessions and in her homework, discovering where she
had been. With the help of her soul she remembered
achievements of which she was proud. Reflecting on
her life's journey, she made incursions back into the
history of her family. This was an important
developmental step for Susan. She was getting rid of
her fear of growing old. In turn, her exercise in
reflection left Susan free to live life more fully in the
here and now. There is an old proverb, "the
unexamined life is not worth living".

An incident just a few days ago raises a question.
Will our souls recognize each other if and when we
meet again? It was during intermission at a concert
celebrating the anniversary of Mozart's two hundred
and fiftieth birthday. The concert pianist was Robert

Silverman. A friend was introducing me to an acquaintance. On the surface I accepted the introduction as a first time meeting. Underneath I felt something different. I'm certain that this woman was having a similar experience. Later on I knew that we had been in the counselling room together. I still cannot remember her name. The cases I report in these memoirs belie the fact that I remember what was said in the counselling room. The question remains. Will we know one another if and when our souls meet once they have merged with the Soul of the Universe? I have doubts, when it comes to clients with whom I have worked at the centre.

It has been helpful for me to record elsewhere how I got to this enviable place in my career. My soul, teamed up with the soul of another individual in counselling, to share such rich experiences. What a privilege. In the counsellor client-relationship the sharing of personal information is quite one sided. All the while my soul is giving to those two clients, Cedric and Susan, at another level. At the soul level the soul relationship is a two way street. When there is progress two souls meet and commune.

My recollections of my work as an administrator come up as positive. There were very few dark nights of the soul in my role as an administrator. A well-nourished soul carried me through. The soul of the Centre, including the team of staff and the board of directors, always came through when the waters got rough. The tough times had money as their focal point. Reinhold Niebuhr would say, in class at Union

Seminary, "pride and not money is the root of all evil." Shortage of money to pay the bills was a problem at times. At those times the members of the staff and board of directors became edgy. In addition to solving the money issues, these individuals needed support and encouragement from me.

There were a few negatives, none of which kept me awake at night. Three situations come to mind as I reflect on those troubling times. One situation involved deciding to cut back on the number of low income clients we could service. Part of our mission was to service clients even if they could not pay. A temporary financial crisis arose for the Centre when the provincial government stopped paying its small grant. At its peak the grant was never more than twelve percent of our budget. Reluctantly, we stopped taking in those new clients who could not pay anything toward their counselling. After six months we not only got back on our feet, but we set up what was called a storehouse fund. We could draw from this fund to help low income clients pay for their counselling. A client applied for the portion of costs between what they could pay and what it cost us to provide the service.

There was a movement afoot in the British Columbia government that encouraged agencies such as ours to involve consumers. This effort had something to do with democratic involvement. Because we were receiving a small grant from the provincial government we appointed a couple of former clients to the board. I had some reservations about this practice. Would clients bring their baggage into the board meetings? Transference (a counselling term about baggage) exploded like an assassins' bomb within our board structure. A former client on the board brought her unconscious issues into the meetings. She wanted to be the treasurer. Our treasurer resigned. Elinor and her husband Don had supported the Centre from its beginning. Another board member whose life's work was related to the military had no understanding of the counselling process. His intentions as a volunteer were honourable even though they were misplaced in this situation. This man joined to support the former client. As the executive director, I had to take the bull by the horns with steps that were not very democratic. My soul provided enough compassion that no one person sustained prolonged hurt. I persuaded the treasurer to come back. The former client resigned. The military type member grumbled and protested, but remained on to complete his term. The soul of the Centre experienced a temporary wound that quickly healed.

There was one set-back for me as the executive director that involved a missed opportunity for the Centre. It happened because the date of an important meeting of the Board conflicted with a commitment I had made to lead a workshop on behalf of the Centre in Northern British Columbia. One of our counsellors, Brenda, received supervision from me in her training. She brought to me a well designed plan which would mean that the Centre would sponsor the first

Employee Assistance Program in the province. We fine-tuned the plan for our Centre. Both of us could see the potential for income that would be over and above our costs. A further benefit would be that exposure through this program would expand our regular counselling services. I assumed that the board would heartily endorse the plan. There were obstacles that I did not foresee. Our treasurer had a beautiful soul in spite of, or because of, physical handicaps. Like many treasurers of non-governmental organizations he was rather conservative with his financial vision. This treasurer advised the board that they should not endorse the plan at a time when the economy was in a slump. I had such respect for John that I maintained my warm feelings toward him. John was supported in his rejection of the plan by our office manager. Carolyn was already working at capacity, always doing half as much again as most would in her position. She did not have the vision to see that there would be enough income from the new service to more than meet the costs of additional office help. Her work-load would have been lessened. These two went to the meeting opposed to our plan. In my absence the plan was turned down by the board. Brenda took the plan to Family Services of Greater Vancouver, which they picked up at once.

My soul not only had to overcome my disappointment. I developed some considerable envy as I witnessed the success of the new program. Surplus money from their Employment Assistance Program was available to Family Services to help pay

for the costs of low income clients. In this situation
my soul had to temper my envy as it was related to
another agency's success. The envy is all gone now.
As I write, feelings of joy and happiness dominate as I
reflect on those years at the Centre.

My soul was nurtured in many ways through
those fifteen years at the North Shore Counselling
Centre. I enjoyed the challenges that I faced as the
chair of the Membership Committee of the American
Association of Pastoral Counsellors, Northwest
Region. The work in that group involved a four year
commitment on my part. Each regular meeting
would take a full day of my time. Special meetings to
Alaska and California for audits of other Centres took
the better part of a week. Meetings with the National
Committee took me to St. Louis on two occasions, and
once to Chicago.

As a committee we interviewed pastoral
counsellors who had prepared themselves for one of
the four levels of membership in the Association. In
some cases an individual would be turned down with
the suggestion that s/he do more work. The standards
were high. Professionalism required that the
committee be fair both to the organization and to the
person being interviewed. Within a short period of
time two areas of my responsibility were spun off to
separate working committees. I pushed hard for this
spin-off, because I found a serious conflict of interest
when a counsellor was found guilty of
misdemeanors. As a follow up to a complaint the
same committee that faced him with the charges was

the one that provided pastoral support to help him work through the process. Setting up a separate committee was the obvious solution. I have witnessed this conflict of interest within the structures of the United Church of Canada. Individuals in the congregation of Bowen Island United Church were hurt and the congregation made a financial sacrifice because a committee of Presbytery got caught in such a conflict of interests.

The opportunities for personal growth were numerous during the years of my involvement in the American Association of Pastoral Counselors. Both my consulting and counselling skills were honed to a level far beyond my expectations. My peers were forthright in their challenges to my suggestions and ideas. I approached those meetings with eager anticipation while driving to Seattle, sometimes in severe winter weather.

There was one incident that embarrassed me. It happened while I was driving down I5 from Vancouver to Seattle. Driving along, thinking about the upcoming meeting, I noticed activity in the car driving alongside to my right. Two women were throwing kisses my way and were behaving in seductive ways. I began to respond thinking that I might as well have some fun. Shortly, I realized that these two gals had a bit too much make up on and that their flowery hats were not appropriate for driving on a major highway. I laughed to myself in my embarrassment. I was fortunate that no one I knew was driving behind me. Further, I realized suddenly what one of my clients was talking about in a recent counselling session. On highway I5 I was the object of fun for a couple of guys out on a drag. Now I had firsthand experience. My next counselling session with Ted, a transvestite, would be better informed.

As an aside, I wonder about the first hand experience of the new Pope. Pope Benedict XVI. He sent out his very first cyclical letter to his Bishops this past week, Sex And Love "Sex without love is nothing more than a commodity". Try selling that on the Chicago Commodities Exchange. Married couples tend to remain sexually active for a long period after the flame of love has burned out. It could be that Pope Benedict is stuck back there in an early stage of development. At the time of his appointment one year ago, there were reports that his choice of career was influenced by his early family relationships.

Firsthand experience is not always essential to be a competent counsellor. I reflect on a situation where I counselled with an older Japanese mother who was in Canada for the funeral of her daughter. This woman could speak no English. Jewel (a name we gave her for the sessions, because of my inability to pronounce her Japanese name) was in a strange country and culture, she had been to the funeral for one of her daughters in a Christian fundamentalist Church. Jewel was unable to make any connection between this experience and her Japanese funeral practices. The rituals had not helped her soul to begin working on her grief. Jewel was in a state of confusion, close to panic. How would she be able to

board a plane and make the journey back home?
During her stopover in Vancouver, another daughter
brought Jewel to me for counselling. Her daughter
acted as an interpreter. Jewel and I made a good
therapeutic connection. She returned home on
schedule where other family members would support
her in the grief process, Japanese style.

One of our counsellors in training had decided to
change his sexual orientation. I was aware of this
when I supervised him during his training. He came
on staff as one of our counsellors two years later.
Daniel had connections with the gay community in
the greater Vancouver area. Referrals of gay clients
increased from previous levels.

It was our policy to see a client twice, and then
present the case to the other counsellors in a weekly
meeting. We usually reached consensus on who
should counsel with a particular client. The
recommendation also included the type of therapy
that would be most suitable. Daniel, our gay
counsellor, brought to our group one disadvantage.
He believed that only gay counsellors could work
successfully with gay clients. He was willing to
compromise his position when his peers confronted
him. Did Daniel have his own unconscious agenda,
like being guaranteed that he always had a case-load?
Our case conferences were both in the interests of our
clients, and of providing opportunities for
professional growth for the counsellor.

Another aside: I have known and become
friendly with several Roman Catholic priests over the

past six decades. Three of those priests found an experiential way of solving the problem of being able to establish a helping relationship with their parishioners. Each of them went to bed with a woman who was not officially a member of their parish. They might have been saved the inner conflict of breaking their vows by better training for their chosen profession. Who is to say that training is better than experience? My theory, as a trained professional, is that both training and experience are good for the soul in any profession.

Another staff situation where there were occasional differences always seemed to get resolved in the best interests of the Centre. Ron Richardson would sometimes say "Mom and Dad are fighting in the kitchen." Ron had a wonderful laugh and fine insight. He became a leading North American expert in Family Systems therapy. My recollections of the resolution of the fights between Carolyn and me are somewhat biased since I was the Dad in those incidents. My best summary is that Carolyn (the Mom in the kitchen) and I became soul friends as we developed our working relationship, our common ground being our total commitment to the mission and work of the Centre. Our managerial skills were at similar levels. We were able to accept that our training and counselling skills were different. No two souls are exactly the same.

Ron and I gradually pursued a different basic approach to counselling theory. Ron took a keen interest in one particular theory. I was quite able to support his interest in the Bowen theory of family systems. In turn Ron fully accepted my more eclectic approach. He too was eclectic in that he could see when another theory would better suit a particular client. Both of us were in agreement that every competent therapist needs to be well grounded in one basic theory without being stubbornly stuck there.

Fifteen years at the Counselling Centre was longer by half than any other position I held over my career. During that last year as the director, the Centre was in good shape financially. It had an experienced and committed staff that was supported by volunteers such as Mary Hurson. On reflection, it seems that my soul was preparing me to look to the future.

While I was away from the Centre for nine months, on a sabbatical leave, the staff assumed the responsibilities that had been mine as the CEO. We had several planning sessions to organize and plan. Individuals took on specific tasks, so that no area would come up short. The plan was carried out with success during my absence. Part of its success was that it included bringing me back into the circle on my return. At the first staff meeting after my return, I discovered that the team was glad to have me back. I discovered also that the individual staff members liked the feeling of power that was theirs while I was away. They were willing to turn certain responsibilities over to me. Certain tasks they wanted to keep. They wanted to continue doing some of the tasks that had been assigned to them months earlier.

To fill the gap in my responsibilities, I agreed to do research in the area of establishing a training program for counsellors. Out of that research, Ron Richardson developed a new training program for pastoral counsellors.

One human trait emerged among staff for the second time in my career. Staff members bring into an organization baggage that is a carryover from the developmental stages of their teenage years. That is the desire to be part of a deep democracy in which the members share power equally but still want a Mom or Dad to take the final responsibility. Members of the staff wanted to hold power while turning the responsibilities back to me.

Reflection informs me that those meetings provided a turning point in my career. Was I resisting their desire to load me with the final responsibility for their services to the Centre? At this juncture of my journey, my soul was pointing me in the direction of retirement. I retired at age sixty-four instead of waiting for birthday sixty-five to come my way. The pull between my soul and the soul of nature would have been a major factor in the final decision.

Years earlier three of us, as leaders at the Atlantic Christian Training Centre, agreed to operate as a trio with equal powers. It was unsuccessful, because who was going to take the final responsibility?

Throughout most of my ministerial career, I had been starting new ventures. Fortunately I was responsible to and supported by a board of directors in each situation. Now I wanted to be on my own in a

situation where my responsibilities would change
direction. It took me more than a year after my
retirement, influenced by the interface between my
soul and the soul of nature, to find the right mix. I
would begin a new venture by growing and
marketing Christmas trees. I would establish a
registered company without any board of directors. I
would do most of the work myself.

My main responsibility has been to my customers
in Massachusetts. Through the growth of my soul
while in West Vancouver for fifteen years, I learned
that my responsibility rested in providing quality
products and good service to my customers. This
would be a basic principle in my new-found freedom.
I miss the support of a board of directors, while
enjoying the freedom of not being responsible to
them. The old principle would be a self imposed
mandate in my new venture.

The journey of our souls informs us that personal
power requires personal responsibility. Your soul
uses your conscience to enforce that mandate. The
Soul of the Universe sets the terms of the mandate.

The Soul of The Universe in Sex Therapy

The development of many souls has been diminished since the days when the early Church fathers, having adopted Plato's philosophy, created an unhealthy separation between the natural and the spiritual world. As a result, the cultures of our Western world have witnessed extremes between freedom and prohibition of both sexual activity and discussion. The extremes are evident when one compares the extent of sex in advertising, the seductive style of dress on the one hand, and on the other extreme, the political correctness about sexual discussion between individuals in social situations. The ambivalence is obvious in the lives of leaders who uphold morality while denying their own sexuality or through absence of openness. They pretend that they do not engage in any form of sexuality. I remember how one American politician got caught in his own ambivalence. He was an outspoken Republican critic of President Clinton's indiscretion, while at the same time was involved in an affair.

The same ambivalence can be seen in the Roman Catholic Church in its edicts about the practice of birth control. We live in a culture where souls are diminished because of this ambivalence about sexuality.

My decision to train to be a therapist arose from problems brought to me by students in the longer term winter courses at the Atlantic Christian Training

Centre. Prior to making that decision I had been giving classes in sex education and answering questions from delegates who came for courses and events at the Centre.

That decision to get training led to my researching the possibilities. The best bet would be to go to Boston University. The six years at Boston University would provide both academic training in the classroom and practical experience in individual, couple and group counselling. The training there was followed throughout the next fifteen years by involvement in several short seminars on sex counselling.

Some of the students at the Centre were mired in a bog of guilt. At the Atlantic Christian Training Centre, both young women and young men came with their guilt about their masturbating activities. I became aware that I needed more training in sexual counselling. Not only did I want to be of more help to my clients. I also wanted to learn more about protecting myself as a counsellor.

I reflect on one problem that arose at the Centre. Two young persons in their early twenties walked across the field to the door of my home around ten o'clock one evening. A winter storm was at its height outside. Elsie and Jason had been caught in bed in a back room of the Campbell house. Sexual activity between students was taboo at the Centre. Eva, the house mother became suspicious and went to investigate. These two wanted to tell me what had happened. They decided to tell me ahead of the house mother. It was important for me to respond to these two with acceptance, understanding, compassion and firmness about the house rules. Here was an opportunity to teach them a lasting lesson about responsibility.

I have written a separate essay about my soul and sexuality. That essay will reflect my openness as well as my philosophical, psychological and theological understanding of sexuality.

If my understanding and sexual development thus flowed over into my soul from hearing the stories of clients, may it be the same for you as you read this essay. I was giving a course to young adults in sex education at the Atlantic Christian Training Centre. Jim stood up at the back of the classroom raised both arms high and exclaimed "What a way to go." Such was Jim's response to my story about how the male bee catches up with the queen bee, mates with her in flight and disintegrates immediately, to drift in pieces earthward.

A high level of trust develops between the therapist and client when sex is the problem brought by the client. Because talking about sex is taboo in our culture, it takes courage for people to bring their sex problems to a therapist. Learning trust and openness in the counselling session was a bonus for me. I became freer to discuss sex as a topic in situations beyond the counselling room.

During my fifteen years at the North Shore Counselling Centre, clients came with a wide range of concerns about their sexuality and activities. Those who came as couples increased my understanding of sex in the couple relationship. The work of souls seemed to get amazing results so long as I kept myself out of the way. Their sharing and interaction in the counselling session appeared to be the medium used by the soul.

One couple in counselling reported that one of their special memories was having intercourse under a waterfall. Recalling that experience they discovered that an ideal and romantic preparation is taking a shower or bath together. Another couple reported that they had been taking turns reading to each other. The woman laid her book on the coffee table, took her man by the hand saying "We've been reading about how sexual activity improves one's immune system. Come with me, I want to improve your immune system."

One couple shared this story. An ideal and romantic preparation for making love back home in the evening was that they had been on a canoe ride down a gentle river when the wild apple trees along the way were in full bloom. The woman talked about the beauty of the many clumps of violets along the banks of the river. The man talked about hearing the silence as they glided along a stillwater.

In the final session with one couple they asked if they could come back in three months' time to report. Here is what they reported. Out canoeing on a smooth lake, a sudden shower came upon them. They paddled to shelter under the overhanging branches of a large birch tree. They sat in silence for a long time as they listened to the rain drops hit the water and splash on the calm surface. The raindrops hitting the surface of the lake made it seem as though nature was performing a dance for them. Nature has its own ways of celebrating. The soul of nature knew in advance where desire was heading on their return to their cabin. I believe that the Soul of the Universe (God) was in collusion with both the soul of nature and the soul relationship of that couple.

Over the past few decades women have been freed up to an awareness and acceptance of their desires and pleasure. This trend has been a real boon to most men. I remember how the men in a couples workshop were subtle in their expectations in this regard. My reflection goes back to a workshop in Prince George, British Columbia twenty four years ago. Lillian (my wife) and I were the workshop leaders. We invited the delegates to split into two groups. The women were to discuss what they wanted most from their ideal man. The opposite assignment was given to the men.

A representative of each group reported back to the total group. One man said that he wanted a woman who could throw the moose into the boat. I took this to represent a setting where the woman was expected to join her man in running the farm. Another man wanted his wife to meet him at the door when he arrived home from work. She was to meet him at the door topless, and holding a tray with a glass of cold beer. Who said what in the separated groups was confidential. You can imagine the fun individuals had in guessing whether or not a specific statement came from his or her partner. Underneath, the whole exercise revealed the depths of the need and wants of both women and men. We were able to talk to the opposite sex without feeling that we would be judged. The format of the exercise and the fun involved freed up souls so that individuals could express their longings. On telling this to a couple in their home years later the wife said "that's me meeting Jim at the door."

I believe that when the sexual relationship is not working creatively for a couple, one of the most important aspects of an otherwise good relationship is missing. When the sexual part has come up short or has been impaired, other elements of a relationship may be damaged. My experience as a counsellor informs me; damaged but not beyond repair. I have counselled with many couples where the relationship has been strained because of a breakdown in the sexual relationship. In a number of situations one or both of the individuals have brought into the relationship problems that had their beginnings far in the past. Parents, clergy, and teachers have been the dominant conveyors of negative messages about sexuality.

Reflect for a moment on the problem brought by Darren and Aileen. Their sexual experience was anything but satisfying. There was no pleasure for either. As a result, desire faded and the candle was about to go out. It took several sessions for us to come to a clear understanding of the problem. In the third session we negotiated a counselling plan.

In a later session Aileen showed me scars on two of her fingers. These scars were the imprint of burns she experienced when she was twelve. Her mother held a burning cigarette to Aileen's fingers. Her mother found Aileen pleasuring herself by masturbating. In the presence of Darren and me, Aileen shared her pain with sobbing and eventual relief. I assume that their souls, the soul of their relationship, together with my soul seized this critical moment of sharing. It was a turning point toward a healthy sexual relationship. Aileen accepted that her sexual desire is natural, given to her by the Soul of the Universe. Discovering these facts of life and love, in each other's presence would have a lasting outcome. Darren and Aileen came to know that they had equal rights to pleasure.

One unexpected situation was the problem brought by Peter and Louise. They had been married three months before they came for help. The problem was that they had not been able to have intercourse (consummate the marriage). That phrase is not helpful for finding a solution to the problem. A phrase likely created by a man who had been denied his "conjugal rights". It did not take long for me to learn that Peter and Louise were not making out. Having identified the problem, I simply encouraged them to talk to one another, using real down to earth language, about how they felt about the problem. Here is what I witnessed as they entered the room for the third session. These two young people were holding hands. Each wore a beaming smile. The overall ambiance was one of a lingering afterglow. No, they did not make out in the waiting room. Travel time would have intervened since they had uncoupled. The glow was gloriously still evident. The soul of a relationship can do wonders. As their counsellor, I had done very little. Most importantly, I kept myself out of the way. They did not need to be told how beautiful it could be. They could find that out for themselves. And they did.

I remember the story of one client who spoke of her experience in a two week workshop. She returned home feeling negative about herself. The intensity of the workshop provided the atmosphere for close relationships. She had intercourse with a delegate to whom she became attracted. She shared with me her disgust when as soon as he had his orgasm he separated himself from her, sat up and lit up a cigarette. So much for a one night stand! Women and most men prefer staying together as long as both are comfortable and nature permits. It is like preserving that delightful experience a kid has when eating a cone of ice cream. I still lick the ice cream to its finish, even decades later. The afterglow can last long after the cone is devoured. The Soul of the Universe gives us that gift of grace.

Experiences which have been reported to me by clients have made an impact on my sexuality. In a whole-life sense, the stories that others have shared with me have made a positive impact on the relationship between my soul, my desire, and my pleasure. The discussions with and stories told by those clients have touched my soul.

My practice in sex counselling will has been underscored by two simple principles. No 1. Encourage the clients to develop comfort in discussing with each other their sexual needs and pleasures. No 2. As a third party in the counselling process, keep myself out of the way.

My beliefs and understanding about sexuality will have impacted my interventions while I counselled with the clients. Those beliefs about sexuality changed for the better as a result of the two way-street in the counselling room. My readers will be able to identify when their experience fits with what I record here.

I would be in the wrong to claim that men and women are similar in their desires and pleasures. Men differ from women in several ways. Both women and men will benefit from discussions with each other about their sexual pleasures. You do not take your date out for dinner and assume that you know what she prefers without asking. She may be allergic to your favourite food. Beautiful souls will feel free to communicate about their desires to their partner.

Both men and women do not like being taken for granted, whether it is for their cooking or their sexual attractiveness and responsiveness. Some of the women were frank about showing their appreciation for their partner. One with a beautiful soul said to her partner "I'm in love with your penis." Another told

her husband "I'm addicted to orgasms with you."
Men respond positively to such affirmation. It is an
effective aphrodisiac. In her sexual maturation, self
acceptance and ability to abandon herself, one woman
told her husband "I've had three orgasms with you
tonight. I'm so thankful."

Men and women tend to have different responses
during an orgasm. Women's earthy verbal sounds
sometimes may sound as if they are being hurt.
Others may sound like they are crying. Actually one
told me that she really cries with joy. These responses
are earthy. That person is caught up in joyful
abandonment.

Sexually mature persons are content at times
simply with the wonderful highs of being aroused
without going over the top; as one woman referred to
her orgasm. I remember the discussion in one
workshop with women in the Bulkley Valley in
British Columbia. The women seemed to be in
agreement that they sometimes became aroused to the
point of no return and then lost it. Their consensus
was, now is not the time to push on. Relax and enjoy
the closeness.

It may be cultural, but I believe that a woman's
erotic zones are not as localized as they are for men.
For some, the whole skin is sensitive to sexual
touching. One woman spoke of how she increased her
sexual response by playing with her own nipples
during intercourse. Men take heed. This has nothing
to do with your lack of manhood or sexual skills. Her
play comes from a soul that belongs to a person who

has fully accepted her sexuality and feelings of pleasure. You do not have to be all in all. Pay more attention to your own soul and awareness. That way you can give way to self-abandonment without worries about performance. One woman reported how, when she got over the fear of self-abandonment, she rode on top of her man singing, "I'm a wild woman now." Her soul had attained a level of beauty and expression.

I believe that men want romance in their sexual activities. A cultural macho attitude has been working against the real nature of men. With women sharing more of the responsibility for being bread winners, men are being freed up to engage in more romantic activities. There is a fine opportunity here for us men to be more romantic, compared with all the heaviness of the bread-4winning responsibility of our fathers.

We need to recognize that most men are not the tough-guy people they sometimes present. The media still fails to recognize their softness and occasional vulnerability. If I open my arms standing in front of a woman and she advances and gives me a hug, I'm in seventh heaven. I am a bit like a cat that rolls over several times a day when you come near him and beckons you to massage his tummy.

The changes in society brought about by the women's movement have been beneficial for men in many ways. Women's increase in their feelings of self-worth, are paying off for men in the area of sexuality. Hearing about a woman's need for pleasure has meant that many men are rising to the challenge.

More and more men report that they are turned on by their partner taking the initiative. I am among those lucky individuals.

A recent experience that I had in early December 2006 is a good example of the pleasure gained from touching and being touched. It is a story I have repeated over the past six weeks. I was just getting out of my car to go up the steps into a small restaurant in rural Musquodoboit, Nova Scotia. Coming down the steps were two couples. They were half my age. One of the women, (all four were complete strangers to me) approached me and asked, "Would you like a hug". With open arms I stepped toward her saying "I love hugs." She gave me what was very much a full body hug. Then she beckoned to the other woman "This grandpa loves hugs. Come Susan and give him one of your big hugs." The men with them stood in awe as their partners were ministering to the pleasure of me a total stranger. No, there was no smell of alcohol. Nor was it a show of disregard for my sensitivities. I assume that these women have beautiful souls. I wonder who these people were, stopping off for a bite as they drove through Musquodoboit late on a December Sunday afternoon. Had they caught the real spirit of Christmas a couple of weeks early?

The senses of taste, sight and smell contribute to increased enjoyment of sex in the couple relationship. One couple shared how over many years they each have the sense of a distinctive taste when they are kissing. They believe that taste is theirs alone. The soul of the couple relationship has put its imprint on their kiss. Not the lip touching kind. I assume that a difficulty emerges when a non-smoker kisses with a smoker.

Developing clarity about each other's expectations is an important task in sexual pleasure. Couples who have difficulty in clarifying what they expect in and from their sexual encounters will benefit from getting their expectations out into the open. I liken some couples who come for help to two sailing ships passing each other in the night. There is no communication between them about the essentials. Their radio transmitters are down. They simply keep sailing on, wondering what is inside that beautiful elegant other as it passes.

A lack of meeting romantic needs arises when the mother is holding a part time job and spends a lot of her time with demanding children. She is the taxi driver for the kids on her days off. Unless her partner takes turns at cooking and cleaning, all desire will have vanished by the end of the day. Such a couple has work to do in sharing their expectations and on correcting the situation.

Have grandpa and grandma take care of the children and go on the occasional holiday. For example, go skiing for three days and find lodging at the resort. Book a room that has a fireplace. An evening following an invigorating day of skiing will offer its own surprises. The couple soul that belongs to these individuals will enrich the souls of each partner. Where is God at this point? Frowning with

judgment and disapproval or smiling over successes
accomplished through the marvels of creation? The
Soul of the Universe must be pleased for having been
partially responsible for how this day evolved.

Sharing these stories with you, I have used
fictitious names for the clients. It is my responsibility
to protect their identity. I discovered early in my
counselling career that trust developed early in the
sessions. I understood the rules about confidentiality
that I was taught. The rule about confidentiality did
not apply to the client. She or he needed the freedom
to talk with others about the experience in
counselling.

I adhered to the confidentiality rules, even when
my professional reputation was at stake due to
incorrect interpretation by other family members or
friends of the client. I recall one attempt by the weak
soul of a professional, who out of jealousy and fear of
my superior training tried to destroy my credibility.
A client shared a conversation with a family member.
The family member shared her version of that
conversation with her pastor. The pastor further
distorted the conversation based on her own beliefs.
Confidentiality prevented me from defending myself
against a misrepresentation of a discussion between
myself and a client.

Confidentiality is essential for a number of
reasons. Most persons take a great risk when they
first open the door to talk about their sexuality. Their
souls will have been more beautiful as a result of

taking that risk. Their openness, desire and sense of pleasure will certainly draw a smile from God.

I came to understand that those men and women who have beautiful souls are comfortable with their sexuality. My understanding is that murky souls do not have the same comfortable level with their desires and pleasure.

I learned from working with clients that in a marriage there are three souls. There are the souls of each person of the couple and the soul of the relationship. One can entertain the idea that there are four souls interfacing with one another, including the soul of God.

PART III

SOUL MONITORS LEARNING

The Soul of a One Room School is Dead

This essay is the story of a soul that died and lives only in memory. Greenwood School was a dynamo for the education of children and youth. The word dynamo best describes the system where teacher and selected students formed a teaching team. The soul of the school encompassed children in eleven grades, a teacher, a building and a property. The students of the school lived within two miles. Greenwood School's soul helped to manage the activities that were significant in the growth and development of the students.

The average annual enrolment was thirty students. Usually, there were students for each of the eleven grades. The teacher would have no formal training at a normal college. The teacher's pay was little more than free room and board in one of the homes in the community. The buildings consisted of an outhouse with a hole in a wooden seat, a wood house and a one classroom building that had a porch. There was a front and a back entrance. The classroom had sixteen double desks and a raised platform on which rested the teachers` desk. Behind the desk was a large slate blackboard. There was a pot bellied stove in the middle of the room. There would be sufficient wood piled around the stove to provide enough fuel for the day. The pile of wood served as a heating pad for the glass jars of soup and stew that students brought for lunch.

Beginning at grade four, I was one of several students who assisted in the teaching of students who were in a lower grade. The teacher functioned as my supervisor. Of the three post graduate schools that I attended through the years, I served as tutor of class mates who needed assistance. Acting in the role of tutor added much wisdom and information to my soul. I wonder if teachers, parents and local school committees of that little school knew how important their system was to the education of their students. In the one room school situation necessity became the mother of invention.

The results from this basic system of education are impressive. My son Graeme, wanting to help with this essay, gave me a copy of an article written by my father entitled History of Greenwood School Section. The article was published in the Truro Daily News on July, 7th 1955. "The Greenwood scholars, under these teachers have made a good showing as they left hoe and went out into the world." In his partial list my Dad names three doctors, two ministers, a bank manager, a civil engineer, a dentist, several nurses and teachers. My Dad concludes "All of the above have given good account of themselves, and many have held important positions of trust."

I learned to love reading books, not from my parents but from my teachers. Several of the teachers in Greenwood School read from one of the classic novels. On reflection, I recall my keen interest in hearing those stories. It was the best part of the day.

We were on our own for finding creative activities outside the classroom. There was no gymnasium or gym teacher. The school property was small, but large enough to pay softball. One year some of us tried walking on stilts. High jumping was quite competitive, but totally unorganized. During the winter months we would build forts from snow and have snowball fights. There was no pond close enough for skating. Coasting on bobsleds was a favourite. One year a group of us would take the noon hour to haul bob sleds up to the top of Benvie Hill and coast down a half mile to the bottom. The road was snow-packed that year, which made great coasting. Another year, one of the students broke a leg coasting on the short road in the woods across from the school. I do not recall any students being obese. The exercise during lunch and recess times, together with chores at home, will have offset the effects of improper diets.

Part of the benefits from our sports was the social development of our souls. I wonder whether the social network of Facebook and Twitter will be effective in preventing obesity. I doubt it.

Opportunities for socializing, apart from the school, were scarce. Going for a week to a Church camp was unheard of. There were no play dates or sleepovers. Going fishing with a friend, swimming with cousins, events such as the basket social at the Temperance Hall in Elmsvale were infrequent activities. My house trailer which is my seasonal home in Elmsvale sits where the Temperance Hall stood.

One of my recurring dreams begins with a long walk along the East side of the school. The dream ends up far through the woods into an open field. It is a place where I have never been before. Travelling through woods involved making the right choices at a fork in the road. When I arrive in the new area, I am not sure of the way back to the beginning. Would I try to go back or move on to explore the new landscape. At that point I wake up.

There are only three former students of that one room school now living in the community served by the school. I become the fourth when I work my Christmas tree lot located in the community. Beulah Flemming was one of those versatile teachers in the school before its demise. Beulah taught three of her sisters. The old schoolhouse is now the residence of a small family.

Summer had just arrived in the Musquodoboit Valley. It was Sunday July 2nd. 2006. The United Church folks from the various Churches in the Valley joined with the Presbyterians at Sharon Presbyterian Church in Dean Settlement. At the luncheon after the service, I approached a familiar figure, Emma Gladwin. Emma had been my first teacher. Her greeting from behind a big smile, "John I was your first teacher. Your first day at school was on your birthday August 30th. You were five on that very first day. That was in 1927, eighty years ago." Surprised at the clarity of Emma's memory I fumbled "Wonderful, and how old are you now. "Oh. John I'm only seventy-nine." was the response with a twinkle in her eyes. I began to explain the mathematical discrepancy in her recall when she said with a smile "I like reversing the numbers. I am actually ninety seven."

As Emma Gladwin accurately remembered, on my fifth birth day in 1927 I started school. I insisted that I be permitted to go along with my sister Frances, who was also heading for her first day at school. My early education through high school was in that one room school. Oh, there was a lobby you entered from the front so that you did not track in too much mud and snow. Hardwood for the pot-bellied stove was brought in from the woodhouse. There was no janitor to do those chores. Throughout all those years the teacher was responsible for all those duties. Usually she assigned some of the duties to students. I do not recall much of what happened that first year.

My youngest grandson Alec celebrated his sixth birthday in early February, 2005. I was with Alec, his Dad Larry and his Mom Ingrid. His Mom and Dad live separately in Kelowna, British Columbia. Alec goes to school near where his Dad lives. At Greenwood school, all grades and ages ended the school day on the same time schedule. Any exception to this would be that of having to stay behind for a time because of misbehaviour, or failing to have done some specific piece of work.

Security at the schools is dramatically different today, eighty years later. My grandson and all his classmates have to be dropped off and picked up at

the door. This practice is because young children may
be kidnapped by a stranger or by a separated parent
who has been denied custody.

At six years of age, young Alec is in kindergarten
in a regular elementary school in Kelowna. The
system can only accommodate him for two and a half
hours a day. One of his parents has to drop him off at
noon and pick him up at two thirty. With both
parents trying to meet the family expenses by
working, that timing is a major hardship. The school
is a top notch one with a good program for those first
year students.

One day, when picking up Alec an old fear
reasserted itself. I felt fear and then I reflect on my
first year at school. The incident which made me
afraid was as follows. My sister Frances and I were
walking home with one of the Eisen girls who was in
grade eleven. As we passed the farm of Neil
Archibald, two farms East of ours, we were chased by
the Archibald's boar pig. We would have been
warned that this pig was dangerous. Years later when
I was a teenager, I was kicked in the face once by a big
steer. I have little fear of animals today, thanks to my
soul.

Although I cannot compare myself with a Saint
Francis of Assisi, the blending of my soul with the
soul of nature has given me a comfort with and a love
for animals. Reptiles are an exception. Fear of snakes
was instilled in me by two factors. Our family had
relatives who moved to California. Stories about
rattlesnakes were part of family discussions around

the dinner table. The Henry family's one time visit back to Musquodoboit, and their regular letters, provided the opportunity for instilling the fear of snakes in me. Also I recall one incident that happened when walking in my bare feet in the pasture near our house. Being barefooted from late May until early September was the usual custom for all the children of the community. Accidentally, I stepped on a large black snake and I shudder to this day at the memory. I have been helped to overcome this fear somewhat by my grandchildren, who are comfortable in picking up snakes. Grandchildren are wonderful teachers. I wonder about the work of the soul passing such characteristics as fear from one generation to another.

I do remember having been held up as a model by my Mom. I could spell the word pneumonia before I was old enough to go to school (as an aside, my Mom was an expert at bragging about her son John). As I grew older the more modest side of my soul was ever embarrassed by this characteristic of my Mom. No doubt she was compensating for the unfortunate event that her education was interrupted by her mother's premature death of, guess what, pneumonia. Bessie Cunnabell Reid died at the age of thirty-eight, after the birth of her tenth child. My aunt Kathleen, the youngest of those children is still alive and is only five years older than I. My Aunt Marg, who died in March 2006 another sibling of my Mother, was a student with me in the little old Greenwood school that first year.

I do not recall which of the older students would have assisted Emma Gladwin in teaching me reading, writing and arithmetic. I would assume that my Aunt Marg. was one of those teacher's helpers. Aunt Marg. went to live with her aunt Madge and Uncle Eben after the premature death of her mother. This couple had no children of their own.

Certain teachers developed a competitive side in their students. The teacher would hold competitions in spelling and mathematics. The first pupil to come up with the correct answer would receive an award, an early form of the game jeopardy on television.

Decorating the school room for Christmas was our only instruction in art. The closest we ever got to lessons in drama was in preparation for the annual Christmas concert. The only ongoing participation in singing was the daily rendition of the National Anthem "God Save the King." As an aside, the only history that we learned was memorizing the Kings and Queens of England. Geography was limited to learning the counties of Nova Scotia and their capital towns and cities. Most of these exercises were intended to hone up our memorizing skills, rather than teach us geography and history. Arbor Day was an import from England. A whole day in May was set aside to work on cleaning up and improving the school grounds. I do not remember planting any trees. The soul of Canada as a nation was in a very early stage of formation. In the Irish theological understanding of soul, Canada has come a long way in the formation of a unique soul.

The life supports of the old Greenwood one room school have been withdrawn. The soul has died. The exercise of reflection will keep the memories alive for a time. Only the souls of people live on. It is time to repeat over the remains of the Greenwood school the words, "earth to earth ashes to ashes." It is a certainty that one day it will be lost from memory. Twenty years ago, the one room building was converted into a residence. The death of its soul was gradual.

New York-Exposed to Greatness: Expansion of Soul and Knowledge

Imagine yourself sailing down the Hudson River. What things in the skyline of New York would you look for? Would it be the Statue of Liberty, the United Nations building, the Empire State Building, Riverside Church, or other buildings of the Columbia University complex? I watched intently for all of these landmarks one June day in two thousand and ten. I was attempting to connect with the soul of that great city as it was sixty years ago.

New York is different today. The United Nations buildings now stand where I served in a little Presbyterian Church sixty five years ago. The destruction of the two World Trade towers in lower Manhattan has changed not only the city itself, but a whole country. President Bush, in a state of the union speech spoke with pride about his determination to remove the destructive element of fear that had overcome the nation. Only two months earlier he was re-elected by instilling more fear among his own people, and then reassuring them that only he could protect them. What is the source of such a man's focus on fear? Does he have a murky soul that is wrapped in fear?

I wonder, would I go to New York today to do my post graduate studies? How would I protect myself from influences of the US culture and political atmosphere? Would I dare to join protestors as I did in Gloucester when we lived in Annisquam? I'm not so sure. These are questions of the soul. The Vietnam war was on then. The president of the Boston School of Theology warned us that the FBI was in our midst. Members of my Annisquam Village Church, even when disagreeing with my position, supported me as their minister. They felt free to discuss the issues with me. I'm not convinced that an equal level of support from that source would be forthcoming today.

My quest for further studies had its roots in my participation in an examination of the Gospels years earlier. My tutors were Doctors Bronson and Archibald, professors in the Physics department at Dalhousie University. I learned to look deeper into the meaning behind the text of the four New Testament Gospels. My feelings of inadequacy as a student minister on mission fields prodded me into making a decision to go to Union Seminary in New York. I had known for some time that I did not wish to be a mediocre minister.

Other incidents and experiences contributed to the process of moving on from one career to another. There was a soul-like continuity and relatedness to that process. The summer of 1947 found me on the farm, and serving as supply minster for the Upper Musquodoboit pastoral charge. Five years earlier I had preached my very first sermon in the little church at Moose River Mines. My Sunday travels to the Higginsville Church took me past the Church where I worshipped as a child. I delivered my sermons in the Churches at Upper Musquodoboit and Higginsville.

The local one room school building in Pinch Gut offered a pulpit and later changed its name to Pleasant Valley. The most exciting memory from that period comes to the fore as I reflect on preparations for my marriage to Lillian Farwell at the end of the summer. As I write, news of Allan Blakeney's death is in the headlines of the media this morning. Allan went to some length to introduce Lillian and me when he and I were friends at Dalhousie University. While he was the premier of Saskatchewan for eleven years he was involved in making important contributions to the larger Canadian scene for example in repatriating the constitution from Britain and in the national health area.

My Dad's beautiful gladiolas would be the flower of choice for the wedding. We would go on a Nova Scotia honeymoon for a couple of weeks and then head off to New York.

Our feelings of excitement and the intimidation of the big city of New York worked together to build our bonding as soul friends in these early days of our marriage. Halifax was but a drop in the bucket compared with the vastness of New York. In Halifax there were no high tech gadgets, such as machines that dispensed hot dishes of food. There was Radio City with its display of early television as a new form of entertainment. A visit to the Statue of Liberty symbolized our appreciation of the United States as a country.

Money was in short supply, and the solution to the problem was to look for work. A visit to a lecture at the Church of the Covenant, which stood where the United Nations building now stands, opened a door. The speaker with a Brooklyn accent talked about "The choich at woirk." Oh what an accent! It touched my soul. My responsibilities in that little Church involved working with the youth, most of whom came off the streets of lower East side Manhattan. There was a young lad from the congregation who assisted me with the program. He was the son of a well known photographer, whose family attended the Church. But I needed additional reinforcements, someone from the ranks of the members of the youth group. I would select and invite one of the boys to help as a junior leader. I chose a tall, lanky lad who was the obvious leader of his friends. One evening, this lad challenged my leadership, desiring to demonstrate to his comrades that he was the boss. My farming instincts came into play. I grabbed him and threw him to the floor. It worked. I had gained his total respect and cooperation. One evening, two policemen came to our meeting. They were curious and were asking questions related to the behaviour of the group members. They asked me to watch the lad I had chosen to help. They told me that he was known to carry a gun and that he forced his comrades to steal for him. The satisfaction of my response to that lad's early challenge has stayed with me. I have never again responded with force to similar challenges. I know that I have mellowed with the years and have learned the skills of negotiation. An important skill is that of making the right decision between using force and negotiating. President Bush and his backers erred on that one in regard to Iraq. When is it appropriate to turn the other cheek, and to walk the second mile? How many American lives would have been saved if President Bush had waited for the people of Iraq to revolt against the regime? With the development of the smart phone and Facebook the people of Iraq would have done the task with less bloodshed.

One of the memorable events with that group of boys was to take them on a one day hike in a park area on the West side of the Hudson River. We got there by public transportation. This journey into the world of nature was a first for every lad in the group. They had never been in the country before. East side New York was their world.

New York was to be my opportunity for learning from and being exposed to some of the giant theological thinkers of the day. My expectations were fulfilled. I studied under the top notch Biblical scholars of the time, Frederick Grant, John Knox and Walter Russell Bowie. Reinhold Niebuhr had a reputation as an academic. It took time for me to understand his thinking. I wanted exposure to him as a person and to his thinking. I recall one of his lectures when he adamantly stated that the root of all evil was not money, but pride. If he were teaching today, would he despair at how important money has become in the free world. Greed would top my list of the deadly sins. Greed understood as striving for more when already you have more than enough. Niebuhr would rap my fingers for the level of importance I have given to money by investing in the stock market.

I soon came to understood that the soul of the city was not the only greatness surrounding me. I was surrounded by the souls of great thinkers who were caring and understanding leaders. Years earlier Dr. Ian MacKinnon at Pine Hill in Halifax was a caring friend who taught me to ski, but he did not have the scholastic ability of any one of these Union professors.

Several years after I graduated from Union Seminary, one of my Union professors and his wife committed mutual suicide. They had been diagnosed as being terminally ill at about the same time. I would assume that they had the support of their significant family members. Their courage is admirable. One would have to know more about the circumstances before making any moral judgment. Hasty judgments that are based on a rigid fundamentalism is unethical, uncaring and mindless. I assume that the McNeill's decision was not hasty, nor was it based on poor theology.

One of the major news items of recent months is about a woman whose soul left her fourteen years earlier and the medical authorities now have withdrawn her life support. The newly realized political power of the fundamentalists in the United States has made this event a big political and legal battle. One Canadian columnist wrote a few days ago that she wouldn't treat her dog that way by, keeping it alive in those circumstances.

Following the tsunami disaster of late 2004 there were many theological questions about why the disaster had happened. Why would God allow this to happen? I was eager to hear the responses of religious leaders on television. The participants were chosen from the major world religions. I was impressed by most of these leaders. It is my opinion the Buddhist and the Roman Catholic leaders came closest to my own theological thinking. I was profoundly embarrassed by the clergyman who was the representative of the Protestant Churches. He was from a fundamentalist denomination in the United States. He was totally insensitive to the other leaders who had stated their beliefs. He chose the opportunity to proselytize the situation knowing that he had a very large television audience. His response was not unlike that of one of the former elders of my congregation in Nashwaaksis. Otis Currie had been a St John River Baptist in his younger years. His message to me on a visit when he was quite old and AIDS was in the news: "AIDS is God's punishment of the gay people of our time." I loved Otis and he was a soul friend while we worked and worshipped together. Otis had a caring and sensitive soul. Differences of beliefs have a place in soul friend relationships.

One of the requirements for obtaining the Master's degree in sacred theology at Union was to write a master's thesis. Lillian was my copy editor. Her English and grammar has always excelled mine. She was always making corrections for proper

English. Sentences and proper construction have often been more important to her than the content of the story. One of my readers was Dr. Frederick Grant. When he came upon a few grammatically incorrect sentences, a style that I had imported from Musquodoboit, he insisted that those phrases were part of me (my soul) and that so long as they communicated the right meaning I must leave them in their original form. I'm certain that neither shorthand nor instant messaging codes would have been acceptable. Such instructions from Dr. Grant taught me to be very cautious when pressured to violate my soul either for linguistic or political correctness reasons.

As a newly married couple arriving in New York for a year of post graduate work we were concerned about Lillian getting pregnant. Young and full of libido we were not interested in abstinence as a form of birth control. A pregnancy would have been a very unwelcome intrusion into our plans. Lillian made an appointment with a family physician in downtown New York. Her request was that this family physician fit her with a diaphragm. After a stern lecture on why it was wrong to use birth control methods, the doctor gave in with considerable reluctance. Could it be that this female doctor was against birth control in principle, but used a diaphragm herself? As late as the early nineteen eighties I was often faced with Catholic clients who practiced artificial birth control, but with some feelings of unease. A conflict within their souls was caused by a Church that has as its

proclaimed mission the nurture of souls. Some of
those clients had not connected the loss of having
orgasms with the unresolved conflict. It was always
enlightening for me when their lights came on. I'm
reminded of Lily Tomlin's delightful invitation on the
program Laugh In: "Ring my chimes."

Riding the subway trains in rush hour was an
experience for reflection. One had to keep a supply of
coat buttons to replace those ripped off in the chaos.
Fifty-five years later the subway system has new
problems. To quote an article in the New York Times,
"Stalls, detours: any wise commuter now knows not
to go into a subway station without a good book".
When I copied that quote my computer insisted on
writing 'boob' in place of 'book'. If you ride a
crowded vehicle in Italy and have good boobs you
may have a problem fending off wandering hands.

Fortunate indeed were those students who were
able to live in one of the apartments in the Seminary.
Professor MacNeil had arranged for us to live in one
of those apartments. Jack and Mary Elizabeth Collins
was another couple who met with such good fortune.
The four of us became friends and exchanged
information until about fifteen years ago when we
lost contact. Mary Elizabeth was a harpist. I reflect on
those times when I helped her carry her harp to
position it in the rumble seat of her car. Another close
association with music that had little or no transfer
into the music side of my soul. I could gently carry a
harp then, but I still cannot carry a tune today.

The Collins and the Stewarts shared a common bathroom that had doors on either side for access from our apartments. I recall going in from our side and finding Mary Elizabeth seated on the loo. She had not fixed the catch on the door. It was a situation that occurred more often than I can recall. Over time, our souls will have risen above feelings of embarrassment. Do souls also become conditioned through repetition?

The soul of the United States is currently enmeshed in fear. Fear of terrorism, fears that Iran and North Korea have the capability of launching an atomic bomb. There were signs of fearful souls in the United States fifty years ago. It was 1959 when Jack and Mary Elizabeth Collins brought a group of older teenagers from New Jersey to the Centre at Tatamagouche, Nova Scotia. These young folk were from Jack's Church in New Jersey. A dominant issue for discussion during that visit was the young people's fear of the atomic bomb. There was considerable concern in the US about the proliferation of atomic materials in parts of the world. They did not have President George W. Bush in the White House to reassure them that he would protect them. When I was a kid memorizing the shorter catechism I thought that God was in control of the heavens, and not the president of the United States. This is another of the ironies of fundamentalist's use of fear. The difference between then and now is in the increase in Bush's political power and the erosion of the separation of state and religion in the United States. Bush appears to believe that his soul is greater than the God he worships.

Living in a small apartment in the bell-tower of a Church near the Seminary was the location of our home for two and a half months in the summer of 1949, when we returned to New York. When I graduated from Pine Hill after three years of theological studies, like all the other graduates, I received a Diploma in Theology. I was advised that if I wrote a major thesis the Board of Pine Hill would upgrade my Diploma in Theology to a Bachelor of Divinity degree. My success with a thesis at Union Seminary encouraged me to go for it. Returning to Union would provide easy access to a great library in the ambience of a scholastic atmosphere. Once I obtained the Bachelor of Divinity degree, the Pine Hill Board automatically upgraded it to a Master's degree. I now had a Master's degree in Theology from Pine Hill and a Sacred Theology Master's degree from Union. It was years later when I would go to Boston University to earn a Doctorate in Theology.

Currently I was the minister of the Boiestown Pastoral Charge in New Brunswick. The salary from the United Church at Boiestown was limited to say the least. There was not a lot of money to cover the expenses of returning to New York. Lillian was able to get secretarial work at Columbia University while I studied. During our time at Union one year earlier she worked for the Waldensian Aid Society, a position obtained through Professor MacNeil and his wife. That position in itself opened her soul to a wider world. During the return visit a year later, my interest expanded as well. A group of alcoholics met weekly in one of the rooms of the Church where we lived.

That summer in New York I conducted the funeral service for one of the AA members. Memories of the actual service have faded. I do reflect with a mischievous smile my recall of my ride across New York to the burial site. I was riding in the lead car of the funeral procession, along with some members of the deceased's family. The hearse was next in the procession. As we passed by Yankee Stadium the brother of the deceased was in the seat beside me. He turned in his seat and called in the direction of the hearse and with a loud voice called "Jim, we're passing Yankee Stadium, take your last look before it's too late." His deceased brother was an ardent Yankee fan. The interest of his soul in the Yankees would equal that of my Musquodoboit minister's excitement over the Boston Red Sox' defeat of the Yankees in 2004. I watched all seven games in the series, two while I was in Vancouver and the others in Musquodoboit. On the night of the famous victory, there were twelve of us watching the game. Three adults, and nine students were from the Musquodoboit Rural High School. One would think that Reverend Gary Burrill had brought in the winning run.

My thesis, produced that summer in New York, was accepted and I was granted a Master's degree by Pine Hill Divinity Hall in Halifax. Little did I anticipate the future, when I would go to Boston

University sixteen years later to work on a Doctorate degree. That's another story. Do you have stories arising out of your reflections on the intertwining of your soul with the soul of a big city? Who are those great individuals who helped to expand your soul?

The Boston School of Theology and My Soul

Earlier today I visited a ninety two year old friend who is in hospital. Bruce has many friends and admirers. He made a statement that had a familiar ring. "John, you are my best friend." I responded to Bruce "Thanks Bruce, that's why I am here. I want to be clear that I'm your friend and not your minister." He knows that I'm the minister Emeritus at the Bowen Island Church. Bruce had honoured me more than he knew. My response to Bruce emerged from my training at the Danielsen Pastoral Counseling Center at Boston University. I had learned to make clear distinctions between professional and soul friend relationships.

My training in the class room and in the internship program at the Danielsen Center in Boston emphasized the need to be clear about professional relationships. There are occasions when it is more important for the pastor or adviser to be a friend and to step out of the shoes of the professional persona.

Just three weeks previous to writing these paragraphs I was invited to speak about my friendship with Bruce. The occasion was his funeral. It was an opportunity to report how much he had shared with me stories about his life as an innovator and inventor. Here was a saint whose best skill was in the practical field. Souls make room for both the practical and the academic. This essay is primarily about my soul and my relationship with the souls of academics. The contributions made to the growth of my soul by friends like Bruce are greater in numbers and quality than those that come from within the walls of academia.

When working with clients, as a counsellor, I often encourage them to reflect back on those individuals who made a difference in their lives. In the context of these essays, I reflect on those people who helped to enrich my soul. At Boston University, three of the professors head the list. They were Dr. Judson Howard, Dr. Homer Jernigan and Dr. Harald Beck. At times each of these academics was more friend than teacher.

Before leaving Tatamagouche in 1965, I had to make a decision about going on for further post-graduate studies. Boston University was at the top of my list of priorities. I wanted to talk face to face with someone on the staff of the Danielsen Center at the University about my goals. Most professors on staff were on vacation. The only name I could get from the Boston office was that of Judson Howard. I called him at home and he invited me to come down from Nova Scotia and meet with him in his home, west of Boston.

The visit with Judson Howard provided much needed information. I wanted to do a reality check. I told Dr. Howard that my biggest concern was starting out on such an important project at the age of forty five. Was I facing reality? Was I too old? I recall how he reached over, patted my shoulder and said "No, not at all. Anybody with your goal and ambition is never too old." I came away from that visit so exhilarated that when I started to move my parked car I damaged one of the fenders moving it the first few feet. I was on cloud nine, but traffic on route 128 soon brought me down to earth. My resolve was made and I soon settled down. Exactly one year later we were on our way to Annisquam and to register at Boston University. I saw a lot of Judson Howard over those years. Some classmates referred to Jud as "Tombstone", because he appeared to be a man of few words. When he spoke it had to be important. And his words were forever wise.

Homer Jernigan and I were born on the same day. We never went skiing together as I had with Ian MacKinnon my Church history professor in Halifax many years earlier. I always felt a kinship with Homer. We were soul friends in so far as professor, supervisor and student could develop that blend of spirit. I learned many bits of wisdom from Homer that I would later apply in counselling. Reflecting back on Homer's influence brings out very clearly how he lit the spark and fanned the flames in the next choice that I made about my course of studies. Initially I had only enough courage to apply for the Master's course in pastoral counselling. Homer invited me to his office to advise me to change the course of my plans, and study for the doctoral degree. In short he was affirming my ability to handle the studies involved. In addition, it was Homer who later on encouraged me to apply for acceptance into the three year intern counselling program at the Danielsen Center. Each year, three new students were accepted for the three year program. The year I was accepted, only two students qualified.

Each intern had his turn at presenting in group sessions with a consultant present, either from the Center staff or the psychiatric community in Boston. For two of my three years I had the opportunity to be the therapist for a couple's marriage counselling group. Initially I was the assistant therapist (which was an observer role), after a couple of months I was moved up to the position of lead therapist. Each group consisted of five couples and the two interns. One of my co-leaders was a priest named Tom. Of interest is that even though Tom was very much a man, the group soon saw Tom as the mother and me as the father in the group.

Harald Beck's specialty was the Old Testament. I signed up for one of his courses "The Cultural Background of The Old Testament." I learned so much in his classes, and was touched by his warmth, so I took steps to open myself for more exposure to him. I had signed up for a ThD. instead of a PhD. for two reasons. First, I had no desire to teach in an academic setting. Second, I would be able to take an additional twelve course points for the ThD. as compared with the PhD. program. As it was I still took several more points than were necessary. There were ideas and information that I wanted in order to be competent in my future work.

Harald Beck became the avenue for some of those extra points. I applied for and was accepted for two direct reading courses under Harald Beck. These courses involved having weekly one-on-one sessions with Harald, to discuss my reading of the past week. What a treat! Two souls met, enjoying this special academic experience. He taught me a lot about blending the personal with the professional. Warmth is an important ingredient of a soul friend relationship. I do not recall discussing his personal life. Yet the relationship took on a personal quality as we shared ideas in the context of discussing culture and religion in the Old Testament.

Now, thirty years later, I feel a surge of excitement as I remember researching and writing a paper about Ruth, Naomi and the wealthy Boaz. That assignment provided a wonderful insight into the cultural influences of two different nations on Ruth. Did Boaz seduce his widowed relative who was gleaning in his fields? Was he inebriated at the time? I wonder if modern advocates of political correctness and opponents to sexual talk in the workplace would take Boaz's behaviour to the human rights authorities. Boaz was protected by the cultural practices and social responsibilities of his time. As a close relative Boaz, in keeping with the ancient Hebrew culture, was responsible for the well-being of both Ruth and Naomi. The Old Testament makes a definite point that both Ruth and her mother-in-law benefitted from the encounter and the cultural responsibilities of their time. Read the story again. Many times at weddings I have quoted the words of Ruth to her mother-in-law about their soul friend relationship. It is a beautiful and enduring commitment. Ruth chapter 2 verses 16-

17: "For where you go I will go and where you lodge I
will lodge; your people shall be my people, and your
God my God; May the Lord do so to me and more
also if even death parts me from you." Ruth leaves
her mother and father and her own people and moves
on in a soul friend relationship with the mother of her
deceased husband.

My relationship with each of these three
professors did not continue after leaving the Boston
area. Ending those relationships was a loss. Yet there
was something more than the skills learned. Each of
them had made an impact on my soul that has
remained part of who I am forty years later. It was
with delight that at one meeting of the American
Association of Pastoral Counselors I met up with
Homer Jernigan. At another meeting I was both
surprised and excited to have a brief visit with Harald
Beck. There is an element of letting go in losing these
important relationships, as one moves on to new
fields. One question I ask myself. Have I put sufficient
effort and energy into maintaining some aspect of
those important relationships? Did Ruth compromise
herself and forget any significant soul mate
relationships that she had back in Moab? Has moving
on and building new relationships compromised
maintaining your meaningful relationships of former
days?

PART IV

SHOW AND TELL
THE INTIMATE SOUL

The Essence of the Family and Change

Love one another, but make not a bond of love. Let it rather be a moving sea between the shores of your souls.

Kahil Gibran: the Prophet

Telling the story of our family from a soul perspective has not been an easy task. Each member of the family would have a different story to tell. Eight decades ago the changes and disruptions to the essence of families were caused by early death, or by two world wars. More recently divorce and separation have become the common factors causing those disruptions. Another major change is that some family members live one third of their lives in retirement. These changes come on slowly and we are surprised by the events. Reflecting on this story brings these changes into focus.

As the patriarch of our family I find myself in the best position to tell that story. A psychiatrist friend has commented on my assuming responsibility for members of our nuclear family. This tendency reaches back to the illness of both my mother and father, and two of my three sisters. Being the eldest son was an influence on my makeup. That family trait is part of our family history. Responsibilities are passed on prematurely to the eldest son. The custom was passed on from generation to generation. The same trans-generational trait showed up in my eldest grandson Micah when his parents divorced.

Genetic, cultural and soul influences all work together to shape our lives and our families.

Community and change are recognized by scholars as two of the constants provided by the Soul of the Universe. As I reflect on the story of our family the one common image I see is: The influence of cohesion (community) was powerful enough to maintain the soul of our family. Only this morning as I write, our eldest son Graeme called to invite us to join him and his Chinese family for supper. We will be eating Chinese food together with his Chinese wife, and their two and a half year old son.

Graeme's siblings have gradually adapted to this change in our family. Because of cultural differences there were occasions when I felt as though I were walking gingerly on eggshells that I did not want to break. The cohesive component of my soul, in common with the souls of other members of our family, has contributed to building a successful family, including the racial mix.

Following our marriage in 1947 Lillian and I were building the soul of this new unity. During the one year at Union Seminary in New York, and the four years at Boiestown in New Brunswick we had limited contact with the families from which we had come. It was a time of building the soul that was our marriage relationship. Graeme was born in our third year at Boiestown. Janelle was born while we were in Nashwaaksis. Larry became one of the family while we were in Tatamagouche. During those years mentors and soul friends, whom I have identified elsewhere, played roles in building the soul of our family. There were peers such as the Gunn and the DeMarsh families in our work settings who laid some of the brick and mortar that helped to cement the emerging soul.

Every one of these individuals and couples were important in assisting our souls in managing the change when we moved from one community to another. From living in a unit with two other couples in the heart of uptown New York City to the isolation of a big old parsonage outside the little village of Boiestown, New Brunswick is an example of the change requiring management.

When we moved from Nashwaaksis to begin and build the new project at Tatamagouche, we were now geographically closer to the families of our origin. Neither they nor we took advantage of what support might have been available for soul building. Other individuals, career peers, community souls, students and staff provided an environment for nurturing and growing the soul of our family. The demands on my time were large those ten years at Tatamagouche. Withstanding those demands the circumstances were ideal for soul growth. It was during that time that I found two of my soul friends. Near the end of that period, Lillian felt some threat, feeling competition from a female soul friend. Had I spread myself too thinly? Had I watered down my role as caregiver? Or had her fear of loss entered the picture? Losing one's mother at the tender age of six becomes part of soul building in a family.

The time and energy for family building was considerably less over the six years in Massachusetts. Lillian was working full time. The children were involved in school and community activities. Our main source of support was the Church community of which I was a part-time minister. There were other student families and couples in the Boston area. I had two families on my mother's side with which we had some contact. Aunt Han and Uncle Ben lived in Plaistow, New Hampshire only forty miles away. Aunt Han was Lillian's mother's sister. Lillian's connection with her aunt became a real plus in the development of her soul. In the mysterious ways of the soul, that relationship helped heal Lillian's wounds caused by her mother's death. Lillian was but a child of six years of age when her mother died. Her tendency to feel the victim faded far into the background during those six years.

There was soul work going on for each of us and for the family as a unit during that time in Annisquam. Part of which is mysterious and difficult to comprehend. I have recorded the parts that I understand. Souls were doing their part in contributing to our growth and managing change. After four years in Annisquam our eldest son moved out of the family and across the continent to British Columbia. The soul of the family remained intact even in Graeme's absence. It was two years later before the rest of the family headed west.

Reflecting on our first two years in British Columbia I am surprised by new insights that emerge during my reflecting. Graeme and Janelle, our two eldest were establishing their own identities. They choose to live in residence at Simon Fraser University. Their souls are part and parcel of their developing separate identities. Larry our youngest, then fourteen, had yet to choose the school he will attend. We buy the house that he discovers with the help of a realtor. I take up the task of building a very new service for the community. There was little by way of a model on which to build this new entity. There were no roots on which to grow the counselling centre except the promise of support and seed money. The requirement of commitment of time and energy was huge. I tried to include Lillian in some of the activities that were related to the new venture. We hosted staff and board parties in our rented home. Later, Lillian teamed up with me as co-leader in marriage enrichment programs. Together, with delegates in those workshops, we explored ways whereby we could enrich the soul of our marriage. Those efforts were inadequate in helping us to find the kind of family support and level of cohesion that we had experienced in Tatamagouche.

The success of the counselling centre was a source of nourishment for me. My relationship with individual members of the board of directors and of the staff (by affiliation this included the staff of West Vancouver United Church) tended to fill the vacuum created by the weakened ties with the family.

Lillian, Larry and I were living in our new home on Burley Drive, in West Vancouver. The house and property were ours. This was the first time that we owned our own home. The property was large. We eventually put a cedar hot tub in place. There were occasional times for soaking in the nude. A few times we climbed out of the tub and rolled in the snow on the lawn.

Once in a while Lillian and I hosted some friends. Larry's choice of friends at his school was from foreign ambassador families who were loaded with money. Financially we were poor. He seldom brought any of those friends to our home. We tried one experiment that might have ended with disaster. We negotiated with Larry to hold joint parties on the same evening in our home. He would invite his friends and we ours. Two girls who were dates of guys in a rival group in North Vancouver came with Larry's West Vancouver friends. The North Vancouver group arrived on the street and then came to our door making threats. The situation was approaching a stage of riot between two rival groups of teenagers. That same year there had been two parties in the community where teenagers wrecked the interior of the family homes. Our guests had reason to be frightened. We chose our elder son Graeme, who was at our party, to go out front and engage the North Vancouver group. In response to Graeme, the group left just before the police arrived on the scene.

Our family had changed. There was little resemblance between this family and the family as it was in Annisquam or Tatamagouche. Following graduation from high school our younger son moved out to live in residence at Simon Fraser University. He tended to return to live at home whenever his finances dictated. The soul of the family was at a standstill, not dead but close to being on life support. My work took on new significance with additional responsibilities as a volunteer in other projects.

Establishing the divorce lifeline program at Christ Church Cathedral in Vancouver was one. About the same time, I was elected as the chairperson of the membership committee of the North West branch of the American Association of Pastoral Counsellors. Fulfilling responsibilities in that organization required that I spend time as a volunteer in cities like San Francisco, Seattle, St. Louis, Chicago, and Anchorage.

I learned that it was necessary to be objective when evaluating counsellors and auditing the programs of counselling centres. On reflection I discover that I was not as objective in assessing the diminishing strengths of our marriage and family ties.

Lillian and I went for marriage counselling. I find it difficult to understand what happened there. The therapist appeared to have skills. Was she intimidated by my professional status? I know that she was not able to give Lillian the support that she needed. We were driving home from the fourth session when Lillian announced to me that she wanted out of the marriage. I was ready to accept because of a growing fear within me. I realized that I was afraid of a future in which Lillian would increase her dependency on me and my soul would be smothered. The wisdom in Gibran's poem on marriage came to mind in increasing frequency "And the oak tree and the cypress grow not in each other's shadow." (I still struggle with that one, now that we are back together. She is caught between her age-related dependency needs and the independence she experienced during our years of separation. I am caught in the middle of her conflicting needs.) My vision of the soul of a marriage is very clear. There are three souls that grow and develop together, while maintaining their own identity. There is the soul of the marriage and the soul of each person. All three souls need room to grow. I believe that the Soul of the Universe is saddened when any one of the three is smothered in the process.

Two factors indicated that the soul of our family was dying and needed some sort of life support into the future. Almost immediately following my moving out from the family home, the pastoral care minister at our Church made a visit in support of Lillian. He had heard the news because of my close association with the Church. As soon as he had left the house, Lillian called me at work. She was crying and in pain. The pastor's poor caring skills had backfired. In his efforts to support Lillian he painted me as an evil person. Lillian was hurt and angry. She felt that she had been violated by his efforts at support. I went to her immediately. I knew about the pastor's poor counselling skills. This was no ploy by Lillian to pull me back into the relationship. Reflection informs me that our souls were at work in that event, teaching us that living separately should provide room for mutual support. That day, the soul of the family managed a process that has continued until this day.

The second factor which contributed in a significant way to the nature of our separation was a legal decision that we made in working out our separation. We selected a woman lawyer whom we both felt could support Lillian. The lawyer worked with a male partner as a team. He recommended that we sell the family home and divide the proceeds. We discussed this and knew that it was bad advice. We knew that Lillian needed the stability of the Burley Drive home. We knew enough about money that it was bad financial advice. We fired the lawyers and proceeded to draw up our own separation agreement. The soul of the family knew something that each of us as individuals did not foresee. Over the next three decades the Burley Drive residence became the focal point for bringing the family members together.

Lillian and I worked together in making decisions about the property and money. I continued to join her for special family events such as Christmas dinner. We developed a pattern of meeting as a couple with friends of old from back East when they came to town. Those times together did not get in the way of my soul making a distinct separation between the Burley Drive residence and my new home.

I was surprised when I discovered that I no longer included the place where I hang my hat as part of my identity. I went through a process of rearranging the parts of my life which inform me about who I am. Where I live is still not an important component of my identity. That remains true for me in spite of a renewed interest in gardening at the Burley property. My interest in gardening is an expression of the lessons taught me by my father in the garden in Musquodoboit. His soul and mine are in communion in the best way they can, reaching across the divide. Each of us is close to the soul of nature.

The residence on Burley Drive has become a meeting place where souls connect and grow. Individuals, including our grandchildren, find this special place as one where the family comes into focus. The soul of the family is healthier now than it has been since we left our roots in the East and headed for the West. Lillian and I decided to live together again, realizing that we need one another. There remain some frictions and discomforting times between those of us who contribute to this family unit. Our family soul does not warrant the endowment of sainthood (I was the Pope during my last year in residence at the Pine Hill School of Theology in Halifax). I feel that my history bequeaths to me some powers for granting sainthood. Read my essay on Saints and Murky Souls.

The reunions in 2005 and 2010 back in Nova Scotia have influenced the soul building of our family. The dividends from investing several thousands of my savings dollars in these reunions are already evident. Those dividends could not be purchased using interest from money in any savings account at my death. There is mystery surrounding the additional factors that kept this family together. I attribute any achievements recounted here to be the work of the soul of the family. Our three children and their children bear the responsibility of making room for souls to influence the families they help to create as they travel the unfamiliar roads of the future.

My dream about being on the mountain, skinny dipping and moving forward naked has been supporting me in remaining open while recounting this portion of my journey. The exercises of reflecting and writing have brought their own surprises. I know myself better, and what I have learned will help me in knowing where I am going along the remainder of my journey.

Soul Making at Family Reunions
Sharing Stories

Have you reflected on your past because you desire a better future? In the TV movie version of Alex Haley's book *Roots*, Chicken George holds his son on his knee saying to him "Son, if you are gonna know where you are going you gotta know where you have been." It was in the year 1995 that I came away from a Stewart reunion in Musquodoboit, Nova Scotia with a dream. The dream began to take form and I started to make tentative plans, and to save money toward making the dream a reality. The dream was that my three children, and their families would come together, meeting with others of our nuclear family, to hear stories involving how they and their Stewart relatives have lived out their lives. My hope was that such sharing would help us as individual souls to know who we are and to develop some clearer sense of where we are going.

The larger Stewart reunion has been held at Stewart Hill every fifth year on the week-end nearest the August 1st civic holiday. This event, with over three hundred taking part, would be too big to accomplish my purpose. With input from our three children and my brother Seymour, a decision was reached to tie the reunion on to the ending of the larger reunion. The first few days of August 2005 would see us gather in Musquodoboit, Nova Scotia.

Our gathering began to take form as "the nuclear reunion of the John Stewart family."

Looking back on our decision about location, it appears that the soul of the nuclear family influenced the choice. We chose a place a couple of miles from where our ancestor Alexander Stewart settled and where he was buried. The location was the St. James United Church and its grounds in Upper Musquodoboit. Our original ancestor, Alexander Stewart, played an important role in the beginnings of the Presbyterian Church in the upper regions of the Musquodoboit Valley.

Finding his gravestone in a heavily wooded area provided excitement for this group of his descendants. Most of his descendants do not even know where this burial ground is located. I had a general idea from a former visit eight or nine years earlier when we had searched for his gravestone, but in vain. His stone, together with other moss covered gravestones, lay under the huge mature white spruce that tower over the cemetery.

A group of us at this first reunion visited the site on the second day. One of my grandsons was removing the moss from a fallen stone at the edge of a small gulch. The group concluded, from the inscriptions on the stone, that this indeed was confirmation that here rested the remains of our original ancestor in Canada. Alexander Stewart had come to make his home in Musquodoboit. Members of this excited group had no feeling that we were in a spooky ghost-inhabited graveyard. There was an

atmosphere of excitement and discovery.
Furthermore, as the day developed there emerged a
keen interest in taking the first steps to restore this
hallowed place. About a week earlier, Janelle and I
rediscovered the obituary of our forerunner in the
Nova Scotia Archives, stored at Dalhousie University.
I knew from a previous search that such a document
had been preserved to inform people like ourselves,
who are eager to know where we are going.

My grandmother Stewart was born and grew up
in Dean Settlement, not far from where Alexander
settled some seventy years before she was born. Our
visit to the old cemetery located on the original Dean
farm booted up one of the few childhood memories
told to me by my Dad. One of the headstones marks
the site where Adam Dean was buried. My Dad told
us what it was like to have a totally blind relative
living in their home when he was a boy. Adam would
have been my Grandmother Stewart's father. The
cause of his blindness was not reported in Dad's
account. His story caught my interest as a child. It
was a surprise to me, partly because I had never seen
a blind person. I wonder now eighty years later, did
hearing that story influence my career decision to
work with people where compassion is an essential
personal quality? In the context of family systems
theory, why did my Dad take into their home one
Norah Dechman (formerly Stewart) when she became
old and frail? The tendency to be compassionate
shows up in three generations.

Our first event that August morning was to visit the cemetery where my remains will be buried. It is situated on the banks of the Musquodoboit River. This is a short walk from the Riverside Church. As mentioned in another essay, that Church community had a major influence on the course of my journey. Many members of my family have been buried there over the past one hundred years, on both my Mom and my Dad's side. For those of you who tend to both deny the fact of your own death and think that your parents are immortal, read on.

Our group of eight walked toward the site that I had chosen three years earlier. To my astonishment, the plot was marked by a piece of board stuck into the ground. On the marker was the name of John Stewart, in heavy print. Since I was not certain about the location, I had requested that a neighbour go with me to identify the spot. He went on his own, earlier that morning, and posted the stake. I was amused by how this scenario developed. I would have removed that marker had I known. I soon discovered that it was not funny for my children and grandchildren. One of them thought that I had erected the makeshift tombstone. She thought that this was odd behaviour on her Dad's part. At an event earlier in life I was nicknamed 'Tombstone'. That was at a laboratory in group development at the Atlantic Christian Training Centre. I was the facilitator in a group of delegates. Because the group was doing a great job on its own, I kept in the background. Their dependency needs prompted them to attach that label, hoping to trick me into more involvement.

Discovering that certain places have souls has been an exciting aspect of my journey. This came into the foreground that morning on August 1, 2005. A quote from Michael Ignatieff's book *Blood And Belonging* is relative to my understanding of places having souls. He wrote after a visit to the Ukraine. There he found that a butcher had used his ancestor's grave to cut meat. The experience led him to write "Land is sacred because it is where your ancestors lie. Ancestors must be remembered because human life is a small and trivial thing without the anchoring of the past. Land is worth dying for because strangers will profane the past."

Too much attention given to the past can be at the expense of the here and now. Elsewhere in these memoirs there is a reference to the basic, unchanging elements in the universe. The need for community is one of some fifteen elements identified by theologians and philosophers. I evaluated how we arranged the sequence of the events at the reunion. Next time I would place greater emphasis on building community. As a starter for the day, visiting burial grounds would be replaced by exercises in community building. We missed the importance of building community by placing too much emphasis on knowing where we have been. Individuals and family groups needed the experience of feeling that they are part of a larger community of Stewarts. That sense of community did not develop until we shared stories over the afternoon of the second day at the first reunion. The three hours of meeting in groups, about twenty persons in each, turned out to be the outstanding aspect of the overall experience. We rotated these groups, thus providing opportunity for all to tell their stories. One large group would have limited participation.

Community building needs to be done without being seduced into feeling so much a community that the group becomes a clique, thus excluding others. I had some real concern about this tendency when I invited the former spouses of my two sons to come. I wanted them to know that they were welcome, and that together we could make people comfortable. The invitation to the reunion included any new partners. It was important to me that I offered to pay for accommodations, and in the case of Ingrid, Larry's former partner, to pay her airfare from the other side of the country. I assumed that these two ex-wives would come, because they were the mothers of my grandchildren. Both women declined for their own personal reasons. I assume that I was in error in thinking that current and ex-spouses would be comfortable within this reunion community. There was so much turmoil in one family structure over my invitation, that one granddaughter left the reunion prematurely at noon on Monday. She thus missed a great opportunity to discover more of who she was at that stage of her development. She is a bright young woman and will eventually discover ways to find the path of her journey onward. "If you are gonna know where you are going you gotta know where you have been." Repeating the advice of Chicken George in the book *Roots*.

There were individuals and family groups that made real sacrifices to attend and to take part in the sharing. I'm convinced that their determination to be there was more than loyalty to my dream. They came because they sensed that there was value for them in coming. Perhaps not even knowing in advance what those values would be.

Many of the stories that emerged in those memorable afternoon sessions are included elsewhere in this memoir. Risking repetition, I want to add one that stands out for me. This story is about an incident that warrants retelling. Underlying the story is a special relationship between my brother Seymour and his wife Fern.

There is a measure of black humour in the manner in which Fern proceeded to get even with her husband. The cause of Fern's anger is not important to the story. Fern was determined to get even. There was a covered well in our woodshed. The punch line in Fern's story is given by way of a picture. She portrays Seymour bending over the well with a lighted match calling down into the darkness of the well: "Fern, Fern". The soul of the reunion reflects the rays of light in the humour of the incident.

I was the oldest person at the reunion, having been around for eighty-three years, give or take thirty days. The stories revealed in a new way how times have changed over my lifetime. I recall the shock of the community of Musquodoboit when one of our single men came back from working in the harvest on the Prairies, and brought with him his Catholic bride.

On Sunday evening July 31st, my son Graeme and his Chinese bride of seven months had a ceremony in St. James Church to renew their wedding vows. They were married on Christmas Eve 2004 on top of the famous Calgary Tower. Sharing in and witnessing Stella's Chinese wedding traditions broadened my understanding of the riches in that culture. It was important to Graeme and Stella that members of his family in the East be able to share something of the commitment they had made to each other. The tradition in many cultures is that weddings are a community function and not simply a ritual involving only two people.

Robin, my nephew, and his partner Doug volunteered to do the cooking for the banquet. A generation back, these two would still be in the 'closet.' The open acknowledgment of their relationship as a couple is more evidence of change. It was also an example of the loving care present in this nuclear family.

The music played during the banquet was reminiscent of the many old time dances I attended during my teens. Gary Burrill, our minister, his daughter Rosanne and Matthew, the son of Dr. Giffin, played jigs, reels, waltzes, and various tunes carried over from the Scottish Highlands. We were back in the days of Alexander Stewart. Following the banquet, we had an hour long concert in the Church sanctuary. A dozen young people provided the music. Most of them were members of the Church band. Six of them formed a choir, singing both modern pieces and a few carefully chosen songs, fitting for those whose journey goes back several decades. One song chosen was How Great Thou Art. Another song that brought back memories was Amazing Grace. Matthew played a keyboard, an instrument that was unheard of in my youth. All of these young people owe much to their music teacher at the Musquodoboit Rural High School.

The school's musical productions and band concerts are of such high quality that one critic claimed about the production Annie "Both the score and the acting was of Broadway quality." The difference between then and now, a time frame covering my eight decades, is to be noted in the training provided and the facilities available at the school. Parents of students raise sufficient money, so that each student in the field of music can have a musical instrument available for training. In the little one-room Greenwood school all grades met in one room. There was no training in music. Even to this day I cannot read music. Was it exposure to classical music while in university, or was it in my genes that accounts for my love of classical music? While my brother Seymour and many others like him who remained on the farm keep their favourite radio station tuned to one that provides country music only.

The story telling exercise was the highlight at the reunion. A family member in those afternoon groups shared a story. That story sparked memories in the group, then someone else would recount a story out of another time period of the family history. The themes of both stories may have had some similarity, but the circumstances differed greatly.

The local general stores were gone, to be replaced by a co-operative. A hospital had been built. Instead of one or two individuals from the whole Valley going off to University, now several dozen graduates move on to more advanced studies. The quality of life for the majority of people in the Valley has improved, as illustrated by those musicians. One needs to ask the question: What entity provides the kind of continuity that accounts for such improvements? Instead of chaos there is progress in the lives of individuals, families, institutions and community. My theory developed over time, and still taking form is that the stabilizing entity is the soul.

I believe, and our family reunion has helped to uphold that belief: souls do grow and develop, yet the soul of a person, of a place, of a family, especially the Soul of the Universe (God), are the stabilizing forces. My soul which embodies, mind, heart (emotions), body and spirit is capable of making contact with, and benefitting from the souls of another person, a place, of nature and of the universe.

When I have lunched with a person, or quietly exchanged reading out loud from a book with another, or listened together to Mozart's Ode to Joy, I come from such experiences saying to myself. "S/he has a beautiful soul." Am I not describing someone who is growing, who has stability, compassion, and loves nature? Someone who has the qualities for being a soul mate with another individual who has some of those same attributes?

In summary, our experience with our reunion of 2005 was both positive, exciting and soul nurturing. There is promise for future generations of Stewarts. One important bit of that promise is the Reunion Cook Book created by my daughter Janelle. That project involved vision, in addition to the work and creativity needed to make it a success. Recipes and family pictures were submitted by almost everyone who came and shared stories. Her vision was looking into the future. Using that book, souls will rejoice from the aroma of fresh bread in the oven. Or the soul's delight may be in looking upon a tastefully set dinner table, and in that first touch of food to the taste buds. At times to be supplemented by a carefully chosen bottle of wine.

Five years later we gathered together at the same location in Musquodoboit. One lesson learned from the 2005 reunion resulted in a change. Everyone was encouraged to show up on Sunday evening for the first session. My daughter Janelle and I planned most of the program. We decided to utilize my previous experience in community building. I used exercises for building community at workshops. Each family was asked to come prepared to share with the total group, important events in their families over the five years since the first reunion. The results were positive beyond our expectation. One family of four presented a short drama to tell their stories. The evening produced several values. There was a value gained in reflecting and telling the family story. Themes emerged providing a picture of the soul of this nuclear family. We were getting to know who we are as individuals and as families. We needed more free time in this reunion for people to interact and socialize. That bonus emerged from the Sunday evening session. Soul growth continued through the next day.

The banquet, the dinner music and the entertainment were arranged in keeping with the 2005 reunion. Robin and Doug catered to the banquet. The music teacher of the Musquodoboit Rural High School and three of his students provided the music. Graeme's daughter Meghan assisted with the dinner music, dedicating her song to Isis, their first child, who was barely three months of age.

Each family was given a CD with a wide selection of family photos. They could purchase, at cost, an album containing the same pictures. Janelle's creativity had been at work for months, getting pictures from more than a dozen of the gathered families. The result was a powerful new tool for reflecting on our past. I recall a statement that I wrote in another essay, "Reflecting is an exercise without words."

The banquet was more than a feast. Yes, we celebrated food while we enjoyed music. We had a holy time in which we remembered those who had died since the last reunion. That spiritual time was important for several of us.

There was a surprise for the author. My eighty-eighth birthday was only four weeks away. Janelle in her thoughtful way had elicited pictures and tributes from my connections over the decades. She presented me with an album that is one of the great treasures in my possession. I have committed myself to review that album on each remaining birthday. Those will be wonderful times of reflection. Janelle knew that it would be wise to present tributes in a 'live' milieu rather than delay until my funeral. There is sufficient of the sin of pride within that I prefer being present to hear the tributes.

The more distant past was not forgotten. Chicken George's advice to his son was not put on the back burner. My eldest child Graeme met with two groups to present information about our ancestry. Graeme has developed a passion for getting information through his research. I admire his desire to back up his findings with documentation. He makes a clear distinction between family lore and history. Documents from courts and registries prove that he is reporting history.

Graeme presented two pieces of information of interest. History records that one of our ancestors who lived in Truro, Nova Scotia owned a property that would be illegal today. Graeme found a document in which this ancestor had registered his legal ownership of his slave. Was the soul of that slave reduced to the category of souls of stones in the Irish concept of souls? Would family systems theorists apply the trans-generational portion of their theory to my family history? That would explain why I was paid a mere five cents an hour for running the edging saw in Kent's sawmill. The slave would have received free food and lodging for his work. I received even less generations later.

Our mother maintained that we had Native blood in our veins. That was part of her inheritance through her mother's father, William Cunnabell. Family records report that one ancestor, an early settler in the New England, was married to a native. Records in Salisbury New Hampshire show that she was in court because she had beat up her husband. In a second document she is hauled before the courts because she was using foul language against her neighbours. Graeme insists that there is proof that this woman was native. There is no documentation proving that her husband was one of my ancestors. There is strong evidence by way of family lore that supports our interest in claiming native heritage. The story supports my belief that there are murky souls among women. The percentage balance between the sexes on violence now measures close to fifty.

Janelle joins me in summing up what we have learned from our two family reunions. A productive family reunion requires a lot of work in the planning. A good balance is needed between reflecting on past journeys and time for building community in the present.

These family reunions would not have been possible without the ancient Hebrew custom of building storehouses for community needs. For each reunion, an amount of fifteen thousand dollars had been set aside to help make the event possible. The skills necessary, and particular soul qualities involved in building that storehouse fund are recorded in an essay on money.

Soul Manages Fear and Greed

I came to a better understanding of the functions of the soul when reflecting on my financial journey. The role of my soul in relation to my financial life involved two of my emotions, greed and fear. My soul impacted each of these emotions. A level of fear can be appropriate in situations where there is danger. Fear enters my life when I am in the presence of some power that I neither understand, nor can control. The soul is necessary for maintaining a balance, freeing us to make good decisions.

Webster's Dictionary describes greed as "an excessive and selfish desire for more of something (as money) than is needed". Greed is one of the seven deadly sins. The Soul of the Universe works in tandem with our souls to prevent our exploiting others through greed.

I became interested in earning money when I was going to the one room Greenwood school. Farm chores and homework filled many of the remaining hours. My brothers and I made time to snare rabbits, which we sold for cash. We trapped muskrats and sold their pelts for income. I ordered packages of garden seeds and sold them at a profit. The money from these ventures was used to buy things that we needed. I remember using rabbit money to buy leather larrigans, the chosen foot wear of the time. The only recall that I have of using money to buy something that was not needed was when I bought a watch as a birthday gift for my cousin Mary. I purchased her gift with money that my Dad let me keep when spreading gravel on the public highway. He let me use his wagon and horses. Even that expense paid dividends. Mary and I enjoyed a beautiful love relationship without any input from sexual intimacy. Our souls were our guardians.

My first experience in investing was when Lillian and I went on a short sabbatical leave from the Centre at Tatamagouche. My soul friend J. J. Creighton advised me to put our savings into bonds while we were away. Those savings were diminished somewhat as the bond market flagged. That experience did not deter me. I sense that my soul had a part in influencing my decision to try again. While in Annisquam, and studying at Boston University, I began to dabble in the stock market. I bought a few shares in a company named Syntex, a pharmaceutical firm that made birth control pills.

When I entered my early fifties I began to think about the future and retirement. With a full time job at the Counselling Centre in West Vancouver, I was now in a position to become more serious about preparing financially for retirement. At the same time I faced the educational needs of my young adult family.

Mutual funds and Registered Retirement Saving Funds became the vehicles in which to grow my savings. I maximized my own RRSP's as the registered funds were called. After Lillian and I separated I continued to put the maximum into spousal RRSP's for her. It was a good investment that developed from the caring side of my being.

Both Lillian and I have been grateful for the part my soul played in fulfilling caring and wisdom in my generosity as a separated husband. Lillian had helped with our finances during those years when I was studying in New York and Boston. She had assisted in lowering our house mortgage when she received her portion of the inheritance from the sale of her parent's home in Armdale, Nova Scotia. Lillian's financial dependency on me over our journey together would disappear. After her retirement Lillian had her own money, which is an important factor in feeling good about oneself. During our years of separation, I sense that Lillian gained a healthy kind of independence that she did not have previously. Handling her own monies was but one medium through which her soul influenced her growth in independency.

It has been an enlightening experience while reflecting on the past, when the soul comes into focus as the dominating factor in coordinating financial planning. I knew that my son Larry had difficulty paying off his college loans. I had no forewarning about how the birth of his son and only child would change their marriage, and Larry's own life. His decisions around his work and his finances were unproductive at times. Did my soul have advanced information about his needs? Was my soul aware that I would be there for him, emotionally and financially? That is a mystery. I am certain that my soul played a role in coordinating my responses to his needs.

I was already supplementing my rather inadequate pension from the United Church of Canada with my Christmas tree business. At one point in time, I was receiving fifty-nine cents extra on the US dollars that I earned from my tree business. As I write, the US dollar is worth less than the Canadian. My plan is to retire from the tree business at the end of year 2012. Will Larry be totally independent financially then? Does my soul know more than I, as I ponder that future?

The extra money that came from Santa's Realtree Farm required careful planning. My decision was to educate myself about investing in stocks. My previous experience was limited. My understanding of the processes and dangers was even less robust. On reflection, my soul was about to monitor the emotions of fear and greed. I turned to my younger brother Leslie for consultation. That move was helpful for a limited time. Then our decision processes about buying, holding and selling stocks moved in different directions. I was to enter a learning curve, which twelve years later requires further reading and self-imposed education. With two new books, the winter months of 2011 will find me involved in an upgrade of my investing skills.

Why am I involved in investing and managing both my own and Lillian's stock portfolios? Does my soul have the answer? Is my soul losing control in its management of my greed? I am hoping that there will be enough value in our own West Vancouver home and pension income to take care of us for a few years in a total care facility.

There appears to be a twofold response to the question that I pose to my soul about my greed. The first part of that response is that my need to work and succeed has crowded out some aspects of my need to play. I have consistently seen myself at a fairly high level of a workaholic. This has changed little over my retirement. The other part of my response is related to the first. I have a desire to leave several small legacies to my children. One of them is financial. To be sure I will have no control over what they do with their share of the legacies. I will have to trust their souls to influence their decisions. I sense that only one of the three children will need support for his retired years. Bad luck and poor planning for his retirement, leaves Larry vulnerable.

With the help of my soul and my interest in numbers at an early age, I have developed an approach to buying, selling and holding securities that works for me. That system is more of a technique than a philosophy. My investment education is focused on reading books, together with articles gleaned by way of the internet. I find one particular newsletter very helpful. The online brokerage service that I use is highly rated. Doing my own research is a self-mandated exercise forced on me because, any time I asked a question about a stock, the online broker at T. D. Waterhouse on the other end of the telephone refused to give advice.

When I do my own research, the information provided by my online brokerage service is better than anything that is available from a financial adviser or broker. Before buying and selling a company's stock, I research the company using a web site where I can study a number of analyst's ratings that are based on past and projected earnings. In this system, I believe that my soul is at work as I adhere to Chicken George's advice to his son about knowing your past. At intervals, I recall the lessons learned from my past failures and successes.

I was concerned during the sell-off in the securities market in the Spring of 2008. I did not lose sleep. I took positive steps to assess our financial situation, including discussions with my son Larry about his ongoing needs.

I had fifty percent paper losses on my small portfolios. Putting fear in its rightful place I decided to take advantage of the situation. It did not take long to regain the paper losses. At the beginning of 2011 those portfolios are up nearly three hundred percent from where they were at their low in 2008. Philips, Hager and North, as managers of our RRIF's and mutual funds is far behind. My soul reminds me that it is easy to be successful in a market that is going up. My soul occasionally gives me a message about the risks of bragging. That tendency has broadened during my ageing. Limited bragging is part of growing old gracefully.

My soul continues to monitor the level of greed and fear that is involved in my financial activities. My soul made its imprint on the book Emotional First Aid Manual which I wrote three decades ago (co-published with the Canadian Mental Health Association). For six years I received income from that manual and from the British edition The Helper's Handbook. A theme running through those books was "helping people to help themselves." Reflecting on my journey has been a positive learning experience. The exercise has been food from the soul indeed.

If Saint Francis of Assisi were to write a review of this section of my journey, what would he have to say? I assume that his soul and mine would have limited similarities. The intertwining of his soul with the soul of the natural world did not include modern financial activities. My soul does not deny the existence of the financial world. I did not go back to the land to escape the emphasis on money in our Western culture. I wanted to re-balance my life.

When I retired in order to be close to nature, I took with me the interest that I had in finances. I came to one fork in the road in choosing my career. One roadside sign read 'money' the other 'people'. Ministering to people has had its rewards. Those bonuses cannot be measured in dollars and cents. My ministry to people and working to build security for the future is part of the balance in a life where the soul is a guiding force.

Soul Interfaces with Desire and Pleasure

*The fundamental task of living both spiritually and
sensually reaches a high point in sex and finds
ritual expression there.*
Thomas Moore - The Soul of Sex.

My soul is the sum total of all of my five senses, my
ability to think, meditate, reflect, pray, project into the
future. My soul encompasses my compassion and my
sexuality. It does not include my physical body except
that my soul uses my body for its own development.
My soul needs me to be responsible in caring for my
body. With my understanding of Soul, it would leave
a big gap if I were to deny the sexual part in this story
of my life.

In this essay I want to be open in sharing with
you that important part of my soul development.
Throughout I want to be respectful of those persons
who contributed to my growth in desire and pleasure.
Any individuals involved in my sexual life were
caring, trusting and responsible persons.

My very first memory of any sexual activity was
being in a closet with two other children, both girls
about my age. I may have been about four years old.
We were examining each other's private parts. No
doubt wondering why our parents were so private
about them.

I recall another incident (that was a one-time
event). Three of us lads, about twelve years old, are at

the river bank after a swim. It was my first conscious effort at masturbating. I do not recall that I made any progress. In any event I have no recollection that any one of us was successful. No sense of guilt or pleasure. That event happened during an extended long term period of latency. All sexual desire was below the surface. My curiosity was satisfied with pictures in Eaton's and Simpson's catalogues. Those pictures of girls in their panties and bras would be poor substitutes for Playboy magazine thirty years later. One of the Church elders in Annisquam thought that I should have a copy. John left a copy of Playboy on my office desk in the Church. The Ladies Aid met that day and got to see it first. No negative results. There was only the irony and humour of the incident.

The early teenage period of latency ended when I became a soul mate with my cousin Mary. There were those wonderful months of a courtship with my cousin. Indeed we were soul friends. Those months expanded into two years. This was a time of exciting personal development, sexually and socially. It was some time before we began petting. There were two drawbacks to proceeding to intercourse. My cousin claimed years later that the main factor holding her back was her mother's influence. The real reason for not going all the way was our fear of the results if as cousins we became the parents of a mentally challenged (retarded was the word then) child. The pill had not been invented. I did carry a condom in my wallet to reassure myself of my manhood. I never did get to use it in our soul mate relationship.

Moving away to university resulted in Mary and I drifting apart as soul friends. We remained friends. Mary got married. I remember visiting her at her home, while she was still in bed after giving birth to her first daughter.

University activities took the place of my interest in desire and sexual pleasure. My motive for any interest in girls during my six years in Halifax was simply my way of guaranteeing that I would have a partner for social activities. I was in a six year long period of latency.

It was in the context of my career development that I now wanted to find a partner. Allan Blakeney and I were good friends. We were on the Pine Hill students' council together. We went separate ways when we graduated. He went off to Britain as a Rhodes Scholar and later became the premier of Saskatchewan. During those last months together in Halifax and before I went to Union Seminar in New York, Allan gave me a great gift. He had been to watch volleyball being played by teams in Bethany United Church. I was invited to go with him to meet one of the players. Following an introduction, Allan challenged me to pursue Lillian, who was to become my wife later, with the intention of winning her from her boy friend. Needless to say Allan was successful in making his intervention into my development. I faced some resistance to my program of pursuit, not from Lillian but from her male date of the time. On a Sunday after attending Bethany United Church, Lillian's boyfriend invited me outside and wanted a physical fight. I wonder now, what the liturgy of the day was that stirred him to pick a fight. It definitely was not that bit of gospel advice about turning the other cheek.

Lillian and I did not have a long period of courting. From the first date until I was to go off to New York to study, we had a brief five or six months to get to know one another. There was little time or opportunity for the expression of sexual desire and pleasure. We had much planning to do, and there was our work to keep us busy. The experiences with my cousin Mary were not forgotten. Instead, with discipline, those wonderful times of play with her were put on the back burner. It was on my 25th birthday, on the night of our honeymoon that Lillian and I both fulfilled our desire and pleasure. Being responsible, the old condom that had been in my wallet for years was replaced by a new one, as we shared in this new experience. I do not like the description "losing one's virginity." I wonder which came first, the term "losing one's virginity" or the early Church calling the mother of Jesus the Virgin Mary? Nothing of soul value was lost the night of our honeymoon.

Our souls were nurtured, and the soul of our relationship bounded onward into new territory. There developed a wonderful interfacing between the soul of our relationship and our desire and pleasure. Throughout our marriage we had a good sexual relationship. It was never experimental. Normal was great. I have learned from my clients in counselling that there is more.

Looking back, variety would have been the frosting on the cake. Lillian's stepmother Mildred approached me about a year after Lillian and I had separated. Along with the characteristics of a kind and generous soul, Mildred had additional qualities. She was a down to earth Newfoundlander who called a spade a spade. Her question elicited a positive response from me. Mildred asked "John was a poor sexual relationship the cause of your break up?" My reply was "definitely not Mildred. That part was good. Just say that we grew apart." I still believe that my response to her was accurate.

Sexual activity is not a necessary component in soul mate relationships. I have slept beside two different women who were sexually attractive to me, without any sexual touching. In one situation we had been hiking in the mountains during the day and returned to our car at darkness. The only bed we could find for overnight was a in a motel where there had just been a cancellation. They had one double bed left. My trusting friend was quick to say to the receptionist, "We'll take it." In the other incident a close friend was experiencing an important loss. She invited me to sleep beside her. The sense of trust led to good feelings about myself. Personal values kept intact, was the reward for all. If sexual activity had developed in a long term relationship with either of those women that would have provided a new level of intimacy between souls. In each of those relationships such activity did not happen. Many years later there remains a caring and loving relationship with one of those individuals.

My soul needed more room to blossom as Lillian and I separated. My story in these essays documents how my soul has developed because of our decision to separate. If we had stayed together, the colour and quality of my soul would have been considerably diminished in comparison with where my soul has now arrived. One obvious testimony to this opinion is the inclusion of the essay on how souls interface with desire and pleasure.

One of my friends is the Reverend Linda Yates. We are not soul friends, although I think that with more opportunity we would nurture a very special friendship. At one public gathering, a Church supper where she was the minister, Linda approached me. I happened to be wearing a pink shirt. Her message was "John I know that you are comfortable with your sexuality." Linda touched my pink shirt saying "That is what I tell Carl when he wears pink." Carl is her husband. Linda lives in an all male household. She is a middle of the road feminist. She knows men well. She and her husband have raised three boys. She has written a book for survivors of cancer, in which she has been very open about her own experience with cancer. She informs her readers how their sexual life was impaired temporarily by the cancer experience. The medical profession misdiagnosed her illness as terminal. Both physically and emotionally, her life became difficult. I introduce you to Linda here in this section for a reason. Linda has taught me and others through her sermons and a book she has written just how significant sexuality is in marriage. Linda's opinion on desire and pleasure (as delivered in her sermon) is that a couple's sexual relationship deepens intimacy and improves communication.

My eighty-ninth birthday is only a few months away. The desire for pleasure remains. My fantasies and memories are gifts from the soul. The advice from the social worker to her parents on her return to visit on the farm was accurate. She had been to a conference on sexuality. "Dad, now that you are old there is bad news and good news. The bad news is that it will take longer between times to get aroused. The good news is that it will take longer for you to have an orgasm."

The change for me is physical. I still need the touching and the cuddling. Friends tell me that I am growing old in a healthy way. I am aware that there is a positive correlation between my physical life among my trees and the level of my libido. Souls, unlike sexual desire, do not go into periods of latency. Souls need opportunities to keep blossoming into ever more fullness.

A few statements in nutshell format sum up my beliefs about pleasure and desire:

God smiles at our pleasure when engaging in responsible sexuality.

Sexual pleasure and desire is a gift from the Soul of the Universe.

The fathers of the early Christian Church deserve condemnation for their distortions, concerning the healthy expression of sexuality.

Sexual activity is a privilege to be enjoyed in responsible ways. It is a gift of grace.

Good sex in a committed relationship enhances intimacy.

Sexual development and the development of the soul, function on a two way street. Each is associated with the other along the journey.

Being comfortable with my sexuality, as observed by my friend Linda, has been a function of my soul. The nakedness in my dream, recorded earlier, suggests to me that I have been true to myself in including pleasure and desire in this story of my journey. If reading my story encourages you to be more open about your desire for passion, we will have been soul friends, if but momentarily.

My Soul Do Take

Now I lay me down to sleep.
Traditional child's prayer

The eighteenth century child's prayer *Now I lay me down to sleep* has evolved into several forms. I was taught the version which reads "Now I lay me down to sleep, if I should die before I wake I pray the Lord my soul do take." That version has the value of teaching children that death is a reality.

The tendency of many adults in our modern culture is to protect children from facing the reality of death. My brother Leslie has a tendency to forget what he was taught in the child's prayer. Aware that some of his peers have died he watches the death notices in the newspapers. Unconsciously he is concerned about death. The denial comes through when he reports to me that a friend has 'passed away.' I witness that he has become part of a modern cultural change in the communities where we grew up. The use of the term "passing away" does not fully acknowledge the separation of the soul from the body at the time of death. I believe that the soul is forever done with the physical body.

Within a soul perspective I have several questions about the circumstances of one's "passing." In what form, physical or spiritual did my friend Evelyn pass through the pearly gates? Were there guards at the gate wanting to see her passport? Were travel plans preordained for her by the Soul of the Universe? Will she return in physical form at some future transformation of the world? Jake, one of my fundamentalist Christian friends, cherishes that belief. Will I recognize and know both Jake and Evelyn in the new world into which they have immigrated? Will Jake remain bald? What colour will be bestowed onto Evelyn's hair? She had a beautiful head of gray hair when I last visited her.

While in this world I can live with those mysteries when pondering my life after death. The questions that I have raised concerning Evelyn and Jake do not reflect a healthy relationship between soul, body and the earthly. I believe that the soul lives on, apart from the earthly. The soul may take with it a distinct feature that reflects the impact of the earthly on its development. But my soul will be separate from my physical body.

Why do I believe that the soul lives on? My experience of God, the Soul of the Universe informs me that God is a loving and caring Soul. It becomes difficult for me to entertain the belief that He cares not at all about the destruction of my soul when my body dies. The Soul of the Universe, who cares for me, has a part in the creation of this my story. I assume that by the medium of my soul, others still alive will be impacted by my story after I have died. Yet there is more. There are other avenues. I remind you the reader of my experiences at the Atlantic Christian Training Centre, when a host of "departed" souls joined me on my walk around the property.

As a Christian I can accept the resurrection of
Jesus' soul. In some mysterious way a few of his
followers experienced some of the beauty of his soul,
shortly after his death. Because they did not
understand the concept of soul sufficiently, those few
followers supported the fact of their experience with
incorrect accounts of seeing the holes from the nails in
his hands and the wound in his side. The empty tomb
is held forth as further proof of their soul experience
with Jesus. Those followers failed to understand the
relationship between the soul and the earthly. A few
years later a couple of the early church leaders
compounded their misunderstanding by totally
separating the earthly and the spiritual as part of
one's journey.

My friend Bruce will soon celebrate his ninety-
eighth birthday. His daughter Reta phoned me
yesterday to tell me that Bruce has been in the
hospital for three weeks now. Reta told me that Bruce
now wishes to join Evelyn, her mother, in heaven. His
wife Evelyn died two years ago. I will be visiting
Bruce this afternoon. I anticipate that he will ask me if
he will know Evelyn when he gets to heaven. Bruce
has faced me with this tough question, at least a
dozen times over the past twenty years. My response
over that period of time has been consistent. "Bruce, it
is a mystery to me, but I believe that the God who
truly cares for you and me has ways for soul friends
to commune in their life after death." Then my
thoughts turn to J.J. Creighton and Don McLean.

I thought little about my own death through my childhood years and on into mid-life. When training volunteers at the North Shore Counselling Centre in West Vancouver I exposed them to an exercise involving their own death. I assumed that in providing support for the elderly, their volunteer skills would be better if they had already faced the idea of their own death. We would all lie on the carpeted floor and imagine our own death and funeral. A couple of times a participant would fall asleep. One man snored loudly thus breaking the stillness of the fantasized death experience. Involvement in those exercises was helpful for me in my journey.

Thinking about where I have been helps me to know where I am going. I am learning about death through messages I get from my body. For three decades I have been getting messages from my body that one day I am going to die. These have not been any external personal threats. I find that there is a relationship between the ageing process and the experience of dying. Dr. Andrew Weil's writing about the division of our cells having a limit up to fifty times has been useful. Dr Weil writes about the Hayflick limit. The human body runs out of its process of cell division that happens in order for the body to be renewed. Furthermore I have been influenced by my loss of friends, my parents, three sisters and a brother.

I want to tell you about two of those losses. My cousin Donald was five years older than I. His family lived nearby and we visited them frequently. Donald developed cancer and was treated and died at home. I would have been eleven years old. I have a picture on the dim recesses of my mind of my cousin lying on a hospital bed in their living room. There was a tube coming from his stomach that was connected to a container on the floor. I thought that the colour of his skin made him look like the Chinese waiters in the restaurant in Truro. I was a witness over a period of months to the slow death of a cousin.

The news about the terminal illness of my soul mate Don McLean six years ago came as a surprise. I was in Nova Scotia when I received a telephone call from a friend in West Vancouver telling me that Don was dying. I talked to Don later that same day (I have told this story in a previous section). My telephone conversation with Don covered only twenty minutes, yet we reviewed meaningful experiences from the years of our relationship.

His life support system had been removed. We talked about his decision to have the supports removed, and how many more hours it would be before he would die. The personal meaning of my experience with Don is important to me because we were soul friends. In addition there was my experience with my Dad. I was with my Dad holding his hand, and having a one way conversation with him, as he died.

I was calm and felt close to the Soul of the Universe in this more recent experience with Don McLean. I had matured in wisdom and my soul has developed over the years since I was eleven years old repeating the childhood prayer.

There is a sequence to the messages from my body and they cover a time frame of twenty-five years. The early ones tended to avoid the reality of eventual death. The first message came with sufficient hearing loss to prompt me to see an audiologist and to get hearing aids. Every two years I get a letter from the department of transportation requiring that my doctor provides a report on my ability to drive. If I deny the reality of that request I lose my driver's license. One year the doctor's staff sent the report to the wrong fax number. Before I resolved the problem my blood pressure hit high numbers. I do not want to lose the privilege that is mine behind the wheel. I enjoy the freedom of the mobility that is mine and the challenges of driving. Subsequent to my 86th birthday I drove from Nova Scotia to Ontario and return. Driving through Montreal, Toronto and Hamilton, six times in all, demanded complete focus on what I was doing. My schedule meant manoeuvring the rush hour traffic in both Montreal and in Toronto. That will have been my last attempt at manoeuvring the rush hour traffic in big cities. I hope to be driving for a while longer. A few days ago I purchased a new pair of prescription glasses to assist in keeping me behind the wheel.

Problems with my joints are another reminder. My experience with osteoarthritis began when I was eighty-four. I dug holes for two hundred seedling trees for psychiatrist friend Jim McDonald at their

farm near Mount Forest, Ontario. It was early May.
The soil was hard and due to my good physical shape
I insisted that I do the digging while Jim planted. In a
couple of weeks, my right knee tightened and became
inflamed. Following a review of x-rays my family
doctor in Musquodoboit told me, "You have terrible
arthritis". She gave me a prescription and the
problem disappeared in two weeks. I met the doctor
with her twin girls at the Musquodoboit exhibition in
August. She asked about my knee. I raised my leg
into the air and said "Thanks to you my knee is great.
Did you tell me that I have terrible arthritis?" My
doctor laughed and said, "I did not. I said you have
treatable arthritis." From then onward, I have paid
more attention to the problems involved in receiving
verbal messages. It is a further sign of the Hayflick
limit being at work. Each passing year my hearing
aids are in my ears more than they are in my pocket.
Only deer have ears in their legs.

I had good vision in my younger years. I bought
my first glasses when I was fifty-eight. I burned those
first glasses when hunting deer. That story is told
elsewhere. It was another twenty years before the
Hayflick limit kicked in and affected my vision. I
began to experience double vision when reading road
signs. With good fortune on my side, I had both
cataracts removed in short order by an eye surgeon in
Halifax. Surgeon Stan George tells me each year on
my annual appointment that someday I will need my
corneas replaced. The cells on the back side of the
corneas are deteriorating. Five appointments along

the journey and with help of prescriptions they are still doing their work of removing water from my eyes. With diligent use of eye drops and ointment I have robbed him of income from two more operations. I doubt if the prescribed medication slows the division of the cells in my cornea. My diligence in using the medication simply takes over a part of the work the cells in the cornea are supposed to do.

It was mid evening and I was walking beside a patient who was doing her daily exercise in the hallway of the hospital ward. A familiar voice came upon us from behind. "John and Lillian, Dermott just died minutes ago". His wife Mae saw us pass the open door of his room at Lions Gate Hospital. I joined the family as they stood around the hospital bed on which lay Dermott McInnes' body. His soul had departed his body only minutes before while his minister was talking to him. Dermott's nightly repetition of the childhood prayer: 'now I lay me down to sleep, if I should die before I wake, I pray the Lord my soul do take,' was answered.

Dermott and I had first met forty years earlier when he was a chaplain at that same hospital. Lillian and I had joined with them in Edinburgh when they were first married. Although he and I were in similar caring ministries we did not connect sufficiently to become soul friends. His work was with patients and their families in the hospital. My work was with troubled people who came to our Counselling Centre in West Vancouver.

We were boys from the farm whose journeys led us into caring ministries. We had been exposed to greatness under the renowned professors at Union Theological Seminary in New York. Whenever he and I connected I felt that we were experiencing a special meeting of souls. Dermott McInnes had celebrated his one hundred and fourth birthday two months before his death. My involvement in that hospital event was more than a coincidence. In some mysterious way souls were at work, even though the feeling of our souls being connected in those spiritual moments in his hospital room was absent. Was his soul busy elsewhere connecting with the Soul of the Universe?

My plans are to continue my work with Christmas trees for four months after my ninetieth birthday. I am still able to do all the tasks involved with one exception. Three months ago I forced my knees to carry loads that did not recognize the limitations set by the Hayflick limit. My pride was the cause of my error. I tend to ignore Reinhold Niebuhr's admonition in the classroom that pride is the root of all evil. My left knee is the victim this time. Loads over sixty pounds are to be left for others. A fifty-five pound bag of fertilizer is still acceptable, two and a half months prior to my eighty-ninth birthday.

I have arrived at a point in my journey at which I must consider my degenerating body and make an estimate of how many more years I have before I will die, as vital to any long term plans. Accepting the reality that I too will die influences much of my planning for the future. In addition to planning for my tree business, there are travel plans, wills, finances, where to reside, and responsibility for family reunions every five years; all of which require cooperation with my soul.

Two big questions emerge at this point in my life. Number one is: what is the role of my soul in helping me to grow old gracefully and to accept the reality of death? I believe that I have answered this question in these essays. Question two is, during this process does my soul prepare itself for leaving my body and joining the Soul of the Universe? I know that my soul has much to do with the first of these two queries. The answer to the second question is as much a mystery as is the life of my soul after it leaves my body. That question remains a mystery, known only to the Soul of the Universe.

Conclusion: Reflections on a Two-Way Road Travelled

The LORD is my shepherd; I shall not want. He maketh me to lie down in green pastures: he leadeth me beside the still waters.
He restoreth my soul.

Psalm 23 *King James Version (KJV)*

Reflecting on the journey travelled over eight decades produced the emerging understanding of the meaning of soul as developed in the essay, *The Meaning of Soul*. The ideas there would rightfully belong here at the conclusion. Instead they were placed near the beginning because the ideas would play a useful function in explaining the connection between soul and the content of all the other essays. It is worth a reread of that essay for a fuller understanding of the meaning of soul. Those conclusions form one of the roads travelled by way of the exercise of reflection. My soul both enriched the journey and grew in its own development, because of the experience of reflecting. In several of the essays the spiral style of writing my story indicates the manner in which the pictures emerged in my mind as I reflected. Translating those pictures into a linear style of writing would have betrayed the ambiance and depth of my experience.

I have reread all the essays with a focus on the role of my soul in shaping my journey. I am so much a part of the story that I cannot be totally objective in rereading it. The exercise of reflecting covering a ten year period of my life became a significant part of the journey. I think that I have been true to my beliefs, my theology and philosophy when reporting on the involvement of my soul in shaping my journey. In sections where telling the story has been intensely focused, producing a range of emotions, I will have been biased when writing about the role of the soul at those particular stations along the way.

Body, mind, heart, family, friends and teachers have played significant roles in shaping the journey. My soul was supplied with an abundance of information to influence the choices that I have made. The choices that I made leave me feeling grateful for the experiences and the life lived along the journey. Writing and deciding to share these essays have been but two of those choices. Author and reader will have joined souls temporarily, if the essays prompt you to reflect on your journey.

Carpe Diem.

APPENDICES

Appendix A

Chronological Order of Events in the Life Of John Stewart

Born in the family home. Musquodoboit, Nova Scotia. August 30th, 1922.

First day at the Greenwood one room school. August 30th, 1927.

Finished grade eleven in June 1937. Equivalent of graduation. No ceremonies.

Left the farm to attend Dalhousie University in Halifax. 1941.

Graduated with a Bachelor of Arts degree in 1945.

Graduated from Pine Hill Divinity Hall, Halifax, Nova Scotia in 1947.

Ordained into the ministry of the United Church of Canada, 1947.

Married Lillian Farwell of Armdale, Nova Scotia August 30th 1947.

Served as a student minister for three summers in rural Saskatchewan.

Bright Sands Mission field 1944 and 1945.

St Walburg 1946.

Studied at Union Seminary New York City. Sept 1947-
June 1948.

Graduated with a Master's degree in Sacred
Theology.

Served as the minister of the Boiestown Pastoral
Charge in New Brunswick 1948-1952.

Eldest son Graeme was born in 1951 while we were in
Boiestown.

During 1949, returned to Union Seminary for two
months to take courses, and to do research for a
thesis.

In 1950 granted a Bachelor of Divinity Degree from
Pine Hill Divinity Hall. The degree was later
upgraded to a Master's Degree.

Served as minister of the newly formed Nashwaaksis
Pastoral Charge 1952-1955.

Janelle our middle child was born in 1953 while we
were in Nashwaaksis.

Created and carried out the plans for an experimental
course at the United Church Berwick Camp Site,
N.S. in the summer of 1954.

Began the work of developing the Atlantic Christian
Training Centre at Tatamagouche, N. S. July 1955.

Carried out a ministry of training laity and providing
retreat programs at the Centre for ten years.

Larry the youngest child was born in 1957 while
living in Tatamagouche.

Taught courses at Pine Hill Divinity Hall in Halifax over the summer of 1965.

Lived as a family in Annisquam Massachusetts September 1965 to July 1971.

During this period his career activities involved:

Six years as minister of the Annisquam Village Church.

Studied at Boston University School of Theology and obtained a Doctorate of Theology degree. The main component of the studies focused on Pastoral Counselling.

Did a quarter of Chaplaincy training at the Danvers Mental Hospital, Danvers, MA.

Trained for two years as an intern at the Danielsen Pastoral Counseling Center at Boston University. Provided one-on-one therapy, one-on-two therapy for couples, functioned as the therapist for couples in groups and provided family counselling.

Involved in a Consultants and Supervisors training group at the Danielsen Center under the tutorship of a psychiatrist.

Worked for a month in West Vancouver in the Fall of 1970 doing research prior to developing a counselling program for the West Vancouver United Church in British Columbia.

Moved to West Vancouver in July 1971 to begin a fifteen year ministry developing what became the North Shore Pastoral Counselling Centre.

Published The Emotional First Aid Manual in 1985.

Published a revised edition in 1988.

Trained volunteers to do community and church work as additional support to professionals in caring for people.

Developed a Divorce Lifeline Program at Christ Church Cathedral in Vancouver as an outreach ministry of the North Shore Centre. This program was modelled after programs in the Seattle area, for individuals going through separation and divorce.

Provided marriage enrichment workshops as an outreach ministry of the North Shore Pastoral Counselling Centre.

Separated in 1983. Lived on board the Gulfstream II, a small cruise ship based in Vancouver Harbour.

Retired in 1986 the year of Expo in Vancouver.

Moved to New Annan Nova Scotia for eight months to check out whether he wanted to retire in Nova Scotia.

Bought into a cabin on Bowen Island in 1987. Shared the use of the cabin, alternately with a second party.

Travelled around the world June through November 1987. Did workshops in Australia and England to train trainers of volunteers. Marketed books to help finance travel costs.

Began a Christmas Tree operation in Musquodoboit, Nova Scotia in 1988. Leased a portion of a woodlot on the old family farm, inherited by his brother. Two years later expanded the tree operation by growing Christmas trees on his own woodlot in Musquodoboit.

Bought a one hundred acre woodlot in Stanburne, Nova Scotia as a further expansion of his Christmas tree business. Moving towards his second retirement, this property was sold in 2002.

Beginning in 1989 he developed and maintained a market for Christmas trees in Massachusetts.

Gradually Lillian and John rebuilt their marriage and began living together in the family home in West Vancouver.

By 2005 the Burley Drive residence became John's home address. Each May until early December the tree operation in Nova Scotia needed his full time attention.

As of the date of this publication the career pattern is unchanged. Health problems related to the ageing process will determine when to quit. Succession problems in the Christmas tree industry remain a factor.

Appendix B

Bibliography

Dorsey, Larry. *Prayer is Good Medicine*. San Francisco: Harper, 1996.

O'Donohue, John. *Anam Kara*. New York: Harper, 1997.

Osterhaven, M. E. "Soul-Advanced Information"
http://mb-soft.com/believe/txo/soul.htm

Ranson, Charles W. "Soul-General Information"
http://mb-soft.com/believe/txo/soul.htm

About the author

In his long and creative life, John Stewart has had many successful careers: as a pastor, executive director of three new non-governmental organizations, pastoral therapist, Christmas tree farmer and author. In each of his careers a main focus was on the training of volunteers who would assist professionals in a variety of community services. Since his retirement in 1986 he established and managed Santa's Realtree Farm, a company through which he marketed his trees in New England. His first book *Emotional First Aid Manual* is a support tool for volunteer helpers. It was co-published with the Canadian Mental Health Association. Following some revisions the book was published in Great Britain under the title *Helpers Handbook*. At the age of ninety he has a few projects in his bucket list. He would like to return to New Zealand and Australia to reflect on his former experiences there. He is planning to paddle and portage a 116 kilometre long canoe trip around the Bowron Lakes circuit in Central British Columbia.

CPSIA information can be obtained at www.ICGtesting.com
Printed in the USA
LVOW100843110213

319464LV00025B/337/P